CHANNELERS
A New Age Directory

CHANNELERS
A New Age Directory

Robin Westen

A Perigee Book

Perigee Books
are pubished by
The Putnam Publishing Group
200 Madison Avenue
New York, NY 10016

Excerpt from *Venture Inward* by Hugh Lynn Cayce. Copyright
© 1964 by Hugh Lynn Cayce. Reprinted by permission of Harper
& Row, Publishers, Inc. Excerpt from *Adventures in Consciousness*
by Jane Roberts. Copyright © 1975 by Jane Roberts. Reprinted by
permission of Prentice-Hall, Inc. Excerpts from *Psychic Politics*
by Jane Roberts. Copyright © 1976 by Jane Roberts. Reprinted
by permission of Prentice-Hall, Inc. Excerpt from *The Unknown
Reality* by Jane Roberts. Copyright © 1977 by Jane Roberts. Reprinted by permission of Prentice-Hall, Inc. Excerpt from *The God
of Jane* by Jane Roberts. Copyright © 1981 by Jane Roberts. Reprinted by permission of Prentice-Hall, Inc.

Library of Congress Cataloging-in-Publication Data

Westen, Robin.
    Channelers: a new age directory.

    "A Perigee book."
    Includes bibliographies.
    1. Spiritualists—United States—Directories.
2. Mediums—United States—Directories. 3. Spiritualism—
United States—Societies, etc.—Directories.
4. Psychical research—United States—Societies, etc.—
Directories. 5. Spiritualism—History. 6. Psychical
research—History. 7. Spiritualists—Biography.
8. Mediums—Biography. I. Title.
BF1242.U6W47 1988   133.9'1'02573   87-29236
ISBN 0-399-51433-3

PRINTED IN THE UNITED STATES OF AMERICA
2   3   4   5   6   7   8   9   10

Special thanks to my soulmate, Howard Brofsky, and also to George Burton, Susan 'Cohen, Audrey Goldman, Sandy MacBride, Ken Maisler, Laurel Marx, Sally Mattson, Claire and Bob, Roger Scholl, Todd Pitock—and my parents, Mildred and Morris Westen.

Contents

. . . The door closed behind them. They climbed out of the earth; and still, climbing, rose above it. They were in the rainbow. Far abroad, over ocean and land, they could see through its transparent walls the earth beneath their feet. Stairs beside stairs wound up together, and beautiful beings of all ages climbed along with them.

They knew they were going to the country whence the shadows fall.

And by this time I think they must have got there.

—from *The Golden Key*
George Macdonald

Introduction
Why Now?

There are as many spirits involved in
the human process right at this moment
as there are human beings.[1]

—Emmanuel

Andrea Torrent leaves her law office in midtown New
York. She is carrying her maroon briefcase in one
hand and an unopened *New York Times* in the other.
It has been a difficult day. Her caseload is burgeoning
and there is a major trial scheduled for the end of the
week. Andrea thinks briefly about her agenda, and
then lets her worries pass. Though her apartment is
only a short taxi ride away, it is Thursday, so instead
she climbs down the littered stairs into the subway
and takes the train to Brooklyn.

The train is hot and crowded with the pulse of people returning home from work, but Andrea appears
cool and aloof, almost as though she is riding above
the car, moving to the rhythm of the wheels against
the tracks. She feels different from the other travelers

on the train, though she knows in her heart they are all a part of her.

This knowledge, "my connectedness to the universe," as Andrea puts it, is new. Only two years old. "It's my glue, my vision, my belief. Whatever you want to call it, I've learned more about this world and myself than I ever imagined I could." Before her current revelations, Andrea insists, "I was fried as an egg. Blood pressure up the kazoo and nerves as taut as rubberbands. I was a screaming mother and a lousy lawyer."

Andrea credits her recently adopted inner vision with buffeting her against career stress and helping her to deal with single mothering. She claims to now "embrace" the world. Included in her ecstatic contemplations is a new generosity. She tithes 10 percent of her earnings to charity, and feels expansive about her donations. "Before I used to worry about having enough money, now it seems to just come to me."

Andrea attributes her new awareness, calm and success to her channeler. As she does twice weekly, Andrea is on her way to Brooklyn for a reading.

Ms. Torrent is not alone in her passion for psychic guidance. During power lunches in California or walks along Wall Street, we are no longer discussing our breakthroughs in psychoanalysis or the benefits of networking our careers. Instead, we're clutching our energized crystals, marveling at our personal astrologer's predictions and espousing our channeler's cosmic vision. An unprecedented number of Americans are now actively pursuing an occult understanding of their reality. Unlike the sixties and early seventies when an almost exclusively middle-class and youthful generation (distrusting anyone over thirty) was attracted to cult and commune, today the wave of Americans who tune into channeling and other psychic phenomena include people of *all* ages, backgrounds and professions.

Board members of corporations, computer programmers, college professors, real estate agents, welders, artists, plumbers, even politicians—many are convinced that knowledge is being relayed from the beyond. So convinced are they that the more devout have left their jobs and families to move closer to the human being they believe to be the vehicle for this extraordinary wisdom: the channeler.

Most who seek a channeler do not have to look too far. Thousands of men and women, many as "ordinary" as you and I, seem to possess the ability to channel entities from the past, the future, even from other planets. Channelers give their bodies over to the spirit, so that his or her knowledge can be shared with anyone seeking it, knowledge many followers feel has changed their lives.

"You will receive what you want because you are the master of your own destiny": This is one of the themes of the popular entity of J. Z. Knight, known as Ramtha.[2] Dr. Peeples, a nineteenth-century physician and philosopher who speaks through the California channeler Thomas Jacobson, assures us that "The planet is a school and every soul is a student."[3]

If Dr. Peeples (or Jacobson) is correct, there must be a reason why, within the last few years, so many "students" are willing to sign up, pay handily (up to $100 for a private session to $1,500 for a seminar) and listen to what channelers have to relay. Spiritual Frontiers, a nationwide nonprofit foundation, claims over 5,000 members. Recently, its seminars have turned from an emphasis on reincarnation (though this subject is still quite popular) to trance channeling. For those interested in developing their own mediumistic powers, there's Free Soul, a psychic training center in Arizona that boasts 25,000 participants. The last time society was swept into a comparable spiritual fervor was nearly a thousand years ago.

Such startling numbers appear to go against the fact that our education is based primarily on scientific and technological explanations. Despite this rationalistic cultural backbone, belief in the beyond is as persistent and pervasive now as it was in the Middle Ages. In fact, our spiritual relationship to the Middle Ages may be more than mere coincidence: It could be a déjà vu of consciousness.

In less than a decade and a half, most people alive today will experience an event witnessed only once before in modern history. The coming of the millennium—the year 2000. Though medieval records are scanty, historians note a dramatic rise in religious belief during that period. In fact, religious fanaticism, it is thought, took its greatest leap around A.D. 1033, the supposed thousandth-anniversary of the crucifixion of Jesus.

Belief in the Second Coming and in an impending Judgment Day may also have given impetus to the Crusades. Perhaps as we glide into the third millennium, we are preparing ourselves for yet another promised Judgment Day. This time, however, we are attempting to explore the world beyond *before* our inevitable entry into it. To help dissolve our fears about death, the channeler Pat Rodegast's spirit entity Emmanuel explains, "There is something remarkably refreshing and educating about dying . . . it is *absolutely safe."*

As reported in a 1984 *Psychology Today* article, Lowell Streiker, a California psychologist who counsels people with relatives involved in occult sects, sees a millennarian thread running throughout our fascination with channeling. "As general pessimism increases, more and more people feel they have no stake in this world," Streiker says. "Occult thought flourishes not so much when circumstances are actually that bad, but when people perceive them as getting worse."[4]

Even if we're not consciously creating a doomsday scenario, we're getting the message. A few years ago, the Associated Press quoted President Reagan as telling the executive director of the American Israeli Public Affairs Committee just days before the massacre of Marines in Beirut: "You know, I turn back to your ancient prophets in the Old Testament and the signs foretelling Armageddon. And I find myself wondering if we're the generation that's going to see that come about."

Reagan's gloomy forecast aside, few of us haven't considered the threat of global nuclear disaster or devastation by AIDS. It's no wonder that so many are reaching to the beyond for a preview of what the spirit world holds.

We are somewhat relieved when J. Z. Knight's Ramtha explains, "There be upon this plane a coming which is called The Close of Your Time. Upon this closing there will be an opening into a Great Age. You have called this age by various names and forms but it shall be called and rendered to The Age of God—The Age of Pure Spirit."[5] We are further relieved when Rodegast's Emmanuel is asked if it is true that our planet is on the edge of destruction and he answers, "School cannot be dismissed so early. The bell will not ring."[6]

Unfortunately, the word was not so promising when noted channeler Elwood Babbitt voiced the spirit of Albert Einstein on November 6, 1971, the day of the Amchitka nuclear explosion: "I am greatly concerned and deeply saddened that I allowed my formula

[E = mc²] to be used by mankind. It was my hope that after its destructive power was realized it would be used in the full measure of good and of helping mankind to construct a more beautiful universe outside of himself, as well as the divine universe that is within the human body.

"I gaze most sorrowfully forward to your coming detonation of Amchitka Island. It is a great concern for all of us here in [the spiritual] dimension. To this very day of your earth time the first atom explosion is still revolving as vibration around your earth. And it is causing the virus infections to human bodies for which medical science cannot hope to find a cure."[7]

Even with the ability of channelers to see into our promising—or grim—future, often followers are more interested in sorting out the disillusionment of their present. Many who look to channeling have also tried Eastern religions, cults and gurus. But what makes the channeling experience so unique is that it also draws the successful businessperson who reports feeling empty despite material gains; the academic who has finally achieved a prestigious position but laments the gap at the end of the goal; those who complain of loneliness or lack of enthusiasm though their lives may be filled with relationships and unending motion.

"I was probably ripe for someone to let me know about the real meaning of life," says Charles English, an automobile dealer from Santa Monica, California. Tall, tanned, with the chiseled features of Kirk Douglas, Charles gives only a hint that life in his affluent beachfront community has been a little too easy in the prominent girth around his waist. Dressed in khaki pants, a black shirt and an alligator belt, the fifty-three-year-old Charles seems an unlikely candidate for following a channeler. Until he shares his account of his steady, anxious "road to nowhere."

"I've been through two marriages and several affairs. Lots of young women, booze, pills, gambling, risky stock market investments, trips abroad, fancy cars, the country club, group therapy, analysis (Freudian and short-term)—the whole bit. But no matter what I did, after a while, I still came up feeling zero degrees inside."

When a woman he was casually dating spoke about her Los Angeles channeler, he first thought the whole idea was absurd. For Charles, life had proven itself just one big vacuous playground, with no reins on behavior, no clues that what happens today matters tomorrow. He had long ago cast aside his Catholic upbringing.

One evening, Charles agreed to join his friend for a session with her medium. What the channeler told Charles changed his life. "My channeler is in touch with several entities, but the one who spoke to me was a sort of Greek mathematician. He knew me, could name specific events in my life. He made a list of all those things I regret most, but that only I know. My dark secrets. And then, he just went right to the point. He said, 'You are the sum of what you do, what you think.'

"Suddenly it hit me like a ton of bricks. I'm responsible! I felt instantly like I was in control—not out of it. But is wasn't like I was thinking about it. It wasn't an intellectualization. It was almost a physical sensation that oozed through every pore of my body. I suddenly felt that I had created everything about me, even my face. It may sound ridiculous, but I oozed *me*. I understood that I was totally responsible. And that meant I could change me."

In 1984 Anthony Brandt wrote in his ethics column for mainstream *Esquire* magazine: "I feel very much alone with my desires, my greed, my hates and fears, the internal pressure to satisfy myself at all costs, and I want something or someone out there to keep an eye on me and serve as a brake on my own will. To keep me humble. To help me accommodate my selfishness to the needs of others and the peace of the world. . . . I still consult the *I Ching*. I find it hard not to believe that a spiritual system of some sort invests the world. Science surely cannot account for everything."[8]

Paul Kurtz, a professor of philosophy at the State University of New York in Buffalo, blames a layman's understanding of science for our recent love affair with psychic phenomena. Editor of *Free Inquiry*, a journal devoted to debunking psychic phenomena, Kurtz is also founder of the Committee for the Scientific Investigation of Claims of the Paranormal (CSICOP), which is composed of a group of scientists, sociologists, psychologists, journalists and even some concerned citizens, all of whom feel it is their responsibility to dampen psychic spirits.

As contradictory as it might sound at first, Kurtz says one of the reasons why ancient beliefs are reaching their present high level of popularity is due in large fact to our recent extraordinary advances in all areas of science. Daily, we learn more and more about the planet's creation. Physicists and astronomers debate black holes, empty space, the big bang theory. It sounds like a science fiction novel as they explain that we are made up of stars that exploded eons ago. They tell us that if we flap our arms on a hill in Colorado, say, it will affect "something" at the other end of the universe. While we're trying to comprehend our place in this vast and almost explainable universe, biologists are creating life in test tubes and altering genetic structures.

"Present-day science," says Kurtz, "seems to demonstrate that virtually *anything* is possible. So people ask why is it not possible for the mind to engage in remote viewing of distant events and scenes, precognate or retrocognate, exist in some form separate from the body, or get in touch with spirits who have passed onto another realm? Unfortunately, there is confusion between the possible and the actual. For many people, the fact that something is possible converts it into the actual."[9]

Gullibility and confusion may account for some believers, but over fifty years ago, Thomas Edison, one of our greatest scientists, was himself convinced that messages from the beyond were as scientifically possible as electricity. He told the *Scientific American* on October 30, 1920: "If our personality survives, then it is strictly logical and scientific to assume that it retains memory, intellect, and other faculties and knowledge that we acquire on this earth. Therefore, if personality exists after what we call death, it's reasonable to conclude that those who leave this earth would like to communicate with those they have left here."[10]

Those who don't agree science is responsible for the sudden channeling epidemic point to the media's recent fascination with the phenomenon. Even in remote areas of the country, belief in the paranormal is boosted by glitzy coverage. Trance channeling probably received the most publicity in 1983 when Shirley MacLaine's third volume of her autobiography, *Out on a Limb*, became a top seller with sales of over 4 million copies. Three years later, her special ABC–TV miniseries based on the book was aired during five hours of prime time, and trance channeling was introduced coast-to-coast to an even wider audience. MacLaine followed with yet another book about her spiritual growth, *Dancing in the Light*.

Book publishers are printing more books than ever

before about the occult. Bookstore owners also report an increase in the thirst for psychic knowledge by their customers. To quench that thirst, an estimated 2,500 bookshops specializing in psychic phenomena now exist in the country. This is double the number of such specialized shops only five years ago.

According to a recent poll conducted by the University of Chicago's National Opinion Research Council, 42 percent of all Americans report they have been in contact with someone who has died,[11] while 67 percent claim to have had experience with some form of psychic phenomena. Further evidence of the widespread belief in the beyond can be seen in another national poll, which indicates that 1 in 4 Americans believes in reincarnation.[12] But can the media be responsible for this? In a December 1986 article in *Time* magazine, Carl Rasche, a professor of religion at the University of Denver, is quoted as saying, "I'm convinced there is some kind of mass hypnosis going on."[13]

If we are under some sort of spell, it seems to be contagious and powerful. Americans who aren't tuning into channeling or other New Age outlets are still craving some sort of spiritual experience. Many are drawn to organized religions that point in mystical directions.

"Never underestimate the ability of organized religion to adapt," Harvard theologian Harvey Cox remarked in a 1987 *U.S. News & World Report* article.[14] Though no mainstream church to date has endorsed the practice of channeling, many religious orders are making adjustments. And those that are find themselves winning converts. The Unity School of Christianity in Missouri is a mystical order that claims it has experienced a 34 percent increase in its ministries and study groups within the last few years. There's also been a rise in faith healing among Episcopalians and a revival of meditation training in Roman Catholic monasteries. Even Jewish mystical practices are on the increase.

The flow of channeling thought is entering into other kinds of practices as well. Sally Mattson, a thirty-three-year-old licensed psychotherapist with a thriving practice in Brattleboro, Vermont, has been seeing channels for her own personal growth since she was nineteen years old.

Mattson is petite and pretty. She speaks in an animated and open way. Occasionally her light brown hair, flecked with gray threads, falls wisp by wisp over her large blue eyes. As she brushes the strands away, her round purple crystal earrings catch the light. On her neck hangs a collection of amethysts and long thin crystals, a half dozen in all. "People," she explains, "have just lately started giving these to me."

Sally feels comfortable in her belief that this is not her first, nor last, time on earth. "Knowing this has freed me up a lot," she says. "It's affected my practice. It keeps what goes on in psychotherapy a learning experience that goes back and forth.

"The knowledge that we are all here to learn has helped to keep me from being judgmental. I really believe people are on their own path and are having experiences that are helpful to them, so I never feel that *I* have the power to know what they *should* do."

Mattson shares an example of how she uses her spiritual outlook in her practice. "If I have a client who comes in, sits down, hangs her head, just stares at the floor and says, 'I'm so embarrassed to tell you what I did—again,' I can reassure her that it's not about judgment. And that experiences are presenting themselves to her so that she can use them to learn and learn and learn.

"Or a client may say, 'I'm so tired of this experience.' If this person comes from a spiritual place similar to mine, which many of my patients do," Mattson explains, "then I can say to her, 'Well, not tired enough!' Then I might ask, 'What is it about this experience that makes it necessary for you to have it again and again?' "

For clients of a less spiritual nature, Sally says she translates this message into psychological terms, a language they can more readily accept.

Though Sally has been open to spiritual answers for over a decade, only recently has she been able to comfortably incorporate them into her practice. "When I used to work at a mental health clinic and a patient would threaten to kill himself in the old days, I would be a psychologist only. I would be looking for the source of the pain in this lifetime. I would try to intervene, and then hospitalize him. Now I handle things differently. The first intervention that comes to me, after I get a sense of whether they need protection (if I have to, I will still do the conservative nine yards), is to say, 'Listen, killing yourself only engineers for you rebirth in your next life of everything you didn't do here—plus some karmic debt.' Of course," stresses Mattson, "I will say this once I've concluded that their expression of suicide is only a measure of their despair, rather than their true intention.

"You see, I thoroughly believe, as channels will tell you, that I've lived before, and if you don't learn your lessons in this life, you have to live them again. We are responsible for ourselves from conception. But there's no point in being fearful about what's going to happen next. It's all a learning process."

Speaking as a professional psychotherapist, Mattson feels that going to channels is a positive psychological experience. "I think so many people grow up being disconnected from their inner voice that they need help in getting back to it. In my view, a good channel does just that. A channel tunes you back inside."

Part
ONE

Prophets, Mediums and Mystics

Long before there were written records, it's likely that mediums, psychics and mystics were helping to guide the less gifted. The Bible offers us numerous accounts of prophets receiving the word of God and sharing it with their disciples.

Before the birth of Christ, ancient Greeks not only employed official oracles, they also relied upon the aid of psychics and "belly talkers." These lay people were said to have spirits who existed within the center of their bodies; prophecies would be foretold through their stomachs. Accounts of belly talkers can be found as early as Plato. Other historical mention of soothsayers dates back to the Roman imperial age, when royalty employed mediums to foresee their future.

Probably our most prolific modern records on the effects and heightened awareness of trance channeling begin in the mid-nineteenth century. By 1854, there were about 3 million devotees in America who believed in mediums and called themselves either "spiritualists" or members of the "Psychic Religious Order."

Within the following fifty years, the spiritualists and their pursuits gave impetus to serious debate and scientific investigation. America became so entrenched in the spiritualist movement that its members made use of approximately 10,000 registered trance mediums. Just like today, they lived in big cities and small towns all across the country.

The Bible

THE OLD TESTAMENT

"Noah received the voice of God: 'I have decided to put an end to all mankind. I will destroy them completely, because the world is full of their violent deeds. Build a boat for yourself out of good timber; make rooms in it and cover it with tar inside and out.' "

Despite the harsh ridicule and derision of his neighbors (because they heard nothing), Noah begins to construct his boat. He listens intently to the Voice and follows each detail of the instructions. As Noah constructs his ark and gathers together the beasts, his neighbors become more raucous, pointing to his project as mere folly.

Most of us know the rest of the story. The flood raged for forty days, water covered even the highest mountains, yet the ark was able to float above the water. It is said that the Lord destroyed all living beings on earth—humans, animals and birds. The only ones who survived were Noah—and those who were with him in the boat.

Noah was a ready recipient for God's instructions. He was a medium, in a sense, but not necessarily a channeler, since he did not pass on information. Moses, on the other hand, did share God's message, although reluctantly at first and in a roundabout way.

It is suggested that Moses suffered a speech impediment. When the Lord spoke to him in Egypt and said, "I am the Lord. Tell the King of Egypt everything I tell you," Moses answered, "You know that I am such a poor speaker; why should the King listen to me?"

We see here perhaps our first and only reference to channeling in the Old Testament: The Lord replied, "I am going to make you like God to the King, and your brother Aaron will speak to him as your prophet." And Aaron did speak the words of God, though they were "channeled" through Moses.

THE NEW TESTAMENT

On the first day of Pentecost, all believers were gathered together in a single house of worship. They were deep in prayer, when suddenly, a loud, ominous noise began to echo throughout the building. At first, the worshipers thought it was only a strong wind. But moments later, they were to learn it was something much more powerful.

"Tongues of fire" spread throughout the house, touching each of the faithful. And then, miraculously, each person began to speak a different language. Simultaneously, their voices echoed throughout the house—they were touched by the Spirit.

Possession by the Spirit and the speaking of tongues is cited again in the New Testament when the prophet Paul visits in Ephesus. It is said Paul placed his hands on a dozen Ephesian men and baptized them in the name of the Lord Jesus. Immediately, "the Holy Spirit came upon them; they spoke in strange tongues and also proclaimed God's message."

In Corinthians it is stated: "The Spirit gives one person a message full of wisdom, while to another person the same Spirit gives a message full of knowledge. One and the same Spirit gives faith to one person, while to another person he gives the power to heal. The Spirit gives one person the power to work miracles, to another, the gift of speaking God's message. To one person he gives the ability to speak in strange tongues, and to another he gives the ability to explain what is said."

Apollonius of Tyana

Apollonius' reputation as an extraordinary mystic was so powerful that centuries later, the Byzantine emperor Heraclius tried to persuade seekers that Apollonius' doctrines and life were even more valuable than those of Christ. In later times, both Voltaire and the British freethinker Charles Blount espoused a similar belief in the Greek philosopher's psychic gifts.

Apollonius was born a few years before the Christian era began. He was a member of the Neo-Pythagorean school of philosophy but was set apart from his colleagues because of his strange and miraculous abilities.

As a young man Apollonius traveled throughout Asia, visiting Babylon and India. While there, he immersed himself in the mystical revelations of the Magi and Brahmins. Tales of his adventures were so miraculous and widespread, they preceded his return to his native Greece. When Apollonius finally did arrive home, he was treated with reverence by fellow philosophers as well as priests.

Although Apollonius insisted he only had power to see into the future, even more astounding gifts were attributed to him, including the ability to speak to those who had died. The most impressive miracle recorded about Apollonius states that while he was visiting Rome, he raised the body of a noblewoman from the dead. It is also recorded that twice he was accused of treason (once by Nero, the other time by Domitian) and was sentenced to death, but that through means never rationally explained, he managed to escape both times. Finally, exhausted from his travels and the controversies they caused, Apollonius retired from his wanderings and set up a school at Ephesus, where he is said to have died at the ripe age of one hundred years.

Joan of Arc

Joan grew up a fragile child in a small village in Burgundy. It is said she had a nervous temperament and appeared abnormally sensitive. Perhaps that's why as a young girl, she preferred to spend much of her time alone and in prayer.

According to the records of her trial, around the year 1424, when Joan was only thirteen years old, she became obsessed with a mission to free France from the English. At that time, she heard the voices of St. Michael, St. Catherine and St. Margaret, all of whom not only urged her on with her plans, but helped to devise them as well.

She convinced Charles, the dauphin of France, to allow her to lead 5,000 men into Orléans, by persuading him of the divine character of her mission. After Charles witnessed a recitation by Joan of a secret prayer, which he insisted was known only to "God and himself," he granted her permission.

Joan of Arc succeeded in entering Orléans; due to her vigorous defense of the French, the English became so discouraged that they ended their siege. Joan stood trimphantly beside Charles while he was crowned King of France, but the real threat to her life was still to come.

On January 3, 1431, she was delivered to the Inquisition for trial. Two months later, she was accused of being a heretic and a witch. Although she was pardoned once, she was soon brought back to her captors and was burned at the stake on May 30, 1431. On December 13, 1909, Joan of Arc was beatified by the Roman Catholic Church.

The Salem Witches

In the year 1692, the town of Salem was not very different from most other towns in Massachusetts. The children went to school, the women worked at home, and most of the men farmed or labored in the town. The Salem townspeople were not strictly puritanical by nature, but they certainly weren't prepared for the power of witchcraft, either imagined or real.

It all began after ten young girls between the ages of nine and seventeen spent the long winter months in the home of the Rev. Samuel Parris, pastor of the village church. Although this might seem the safest of all places for young girls to keep out of mischief, it wasn't. During this time, they were suspected of learning magic tricks, palmistry and trancelike states from Pastor Parris's West Indian slave, Tituba.

The girls, perhaps influenced by rumors of witchcraft in the town and fearful of their own spiritual health, reported their activities to Pastor Parris and accused Tituba and two other older women of bewitching them.

The charges of bewitchment spread rapidly, and before long many more women were accused. Trials were conducted in accordance with the English law of the time, although many of them were eerie and reeked of hysteria and the supernatural. Often those accused, or witnesses who feared they were be-witched, would speak in strange languages or with voices other than their own. Within four months, hundreds of Salem inhabitants were accused of witch-craft. Nineteen were eventually hanged.

Emanuel Swedenborg

The idea that people could communicate with the departed began to generate wide interest and respectability when Emanuel Swedenborg (1688–1772), a Swedish scientist, began to preach that he could make contact with the dead and bring forth messages from them. Some spiritualists, in fact, claim Swedenborg is the father of our knowledge of supernatural matters.

Swedenborg was a man for all seasons. He was renowned as a brilliant mining and military engineer and as an authority on metallurgy. He was also a great authority on astronomy and physics and wrote extensively about the power of the ocean's tides and the determination of latitude. To this already vast knowledge he added his expertise in zoology, anatomy, finance and political economics. But perhaps most relevantly, Swedenborg was a profound Biblical scholar who was taught theology at the earliest age by his father, a devout Lutheran pastor.

Even as a young boy Swedenborg had visionary moments, but his psychic powers didn't blossom to their full intensity until he reached the age of fifty-five. Around this time, he began to live his life simply, almost monastically. His diet consisted chiefly of bread and milk as well as large quantities of coffee. He paid no attention to the distinction between day and night, and sometimes lay for days in a trance, while his servants were disturbed in the evenings with what Swedenborg called "conflicts with evil spirits."[1]

More often, Swedenborg would communicate with the beyond, during the day, quite civilly and calmly, with all his faculties functioning. But when he communed with spirits he would hardly draw a breath for hours at a time. Or, as he himself stated, "would take in only enough air to serve as a supply to the spirit's thoughts."[2]

Among his innumerable disclosures, Swedenborg found that the other world, to which we all go after death, consists of a number of different spheres representing various shades of luminosity and happiness, each of us going to the spiritual condition that most fits our individual needs. Swedenborg also reported that death was made easy because of the presence of celestial beings who helped the newcomer into his fresh existence. Following the initial welcome, newcomers have an immediate period of rest and regain consciousness in a few days.

Today, there are still followers of Swedenborg throughout the world.

Andrew Jackson Davis

Andrew Jackson Davis is thought by many to be one of the most gifted trance mediums in the history of American spiritualism. He was born in 1826 along the Hudson. His mother was a visionary who attributed her powers to superstitious reasoning. His father was an alcoholic laborer. Davis grew up starved for both nutritional and emotional nourishment. His parents disapproved of education, and it wasn't until the age of sixteen that Andrew saw his first book.

Davis's psychic powers began to develop in his later boyhood. Like Joan of Arc, while taking long solitary walks in the woods, he heard voices that gave him advice and comfort. He also became clairvoyant, and at the time of his mother's death had a vision of a beautiful home in a land of brightness that he was certain was his mother's resting place.

For a while, Davis lent his visionary ability to medical diagnosis. He described how the human body became transparent to his spirit eye, which seemed to emanate from the center of his forehead. Each organ, he reported, stood out clearly and with a special radiance of its own, except when dimmed by disease.

Though completely uneducated, Davis was so in touch with spiritual forces that at the age of twenty he wrote a highly acclaimed book of philosophy entitled *Principles of Nature*. He predicted an Age of Spiritualism in the following passage:

> "It is true that spirits commune with one another while one is in the body and the other in the higher spheres—and this, too, when the person in the body is unconscious of the influx, and hence cannot be convinced of the fact; and this truth will ere long present itself in the form of a living demonstration. And the world will hail with delight the ushering in of that era when the interiors of men will be opened, and the spiritual communion will be established."[3]

D. D. Home

In 1833, Daniel Dunglas Home was born into a privileged family in Currie, England. It is said he was a distant relation of the Earl of Home.

Even as a child, Home exhibited psychic faculties. Around the age of thirteen, he allegedly made a pact with his best friend, Edwin, that whoever should die first would return to tell the other of the world beyond. The next day, Home and his family moved to another district. One month later, just after retiring to bed, Home had a vision of his friend's death and announced it to his aunt. Two days later, she received the news officially, via a letter brought by coach.

As Home's mediumship became more attuned, he traveled from town to town, giving as many as seven séances a day even though they proved to drain his physical strength. Word of his remarkable capabilities spread to America, and the poet William Cullen Bryant, accompanied by a professor from Harvard, attended sessions with Home in England.

Home sailed to New York, and on his arrival met many distinguished spiritualists of the day, including several university professors and a judge of the New York Supreme Court, all of whom attested to his mediumistic powers.

On his return to England, Home's physical health continued to deteriorate. He existed with no income and refused to take any money for his séances, saying: "I have been sent on a mission to demonstrate immortality. I have never taken money for it, and I never will."

Listed among Home's exceptional gifts was his ability to levitate. There are over one hundred eyewitness accounts of his feats. One such report dates from the summer of 1857. It states simply: "In a château near Bordeaux, in the presence of Madame Ducos, widow of the Minister of Marine, and the Count and Countess de Beaumont, Home was lifted to the ceiling of a lofty room."[4]

Margaret and Katherine Fox

When the Fox sisters moved in 1847 to their new home in Hydesville, New York, they gave up playing with dolls. Their interests turned to the rappings and other noises they heard throughout their house—an old house many residents in the area claimed was haunted. But oddly enough, the strange sounds seemed to occur only when Margaret, thirteen, and Katherine, eleven, were present. Their distraught mother was certain that spirits from the beyond were trying to get in touch with her family through her innocent children.

When neighbors heard about the sisters' special ability they came to the Fox house, bringing with them questions they wanted to ask the spirits. Sure enough, after every question there came a "rapped" answer.

Before long, the two sisters were convinced that the ghost who was using them as mediums was really a poor soul who had been murdered in the house and was unable to rest in peace. When the police searched the old house and discovered some human bones in the basement, it was widely assumed they belonged to the murder victim. But the discovery of these physical remains did not leave the Fox family in peace. They next claimed to hear even more disturbing noises, including a body being dragged across the floor. Driven out by the raucous spirits, the Fox family packed up and left Hydesville for Rochester.

Unfortunately, they were not to find a "Home Sweet Home" in Rochester, either. The rappings continued and their new home became a meeting hall for spiritualists and seekers from all over the country.

Leah Fish, their older sister, arranged for Margaret and Katherine to get money in return for their communications with the beyond. A system was devised whereby the client could ask a question, then go through the alphabet until the rapping was heard. Messages from the beyond were thereby spelled out letter by letter, word for word.

The sisters' ability to communicate with other worlds was heightened and they took their psychic gifts on the road. They had by now perfected a new system that included the gift of contacting such historical personalities as John Calhoun and Benjamin Franklin.

Committees of skeptics would routinely try to discredit the girls' exceptional gifts, but for quite a while their inquiries led nowhere. Eventually, doctors did find that the girls were able to make the rapping noises by cracking their knee joints—but many occultists believe the doctors' diagnosis was never satisfactorily proven.

The Eddy Family

In a secluded valley in the Green Mountains of Vermont, during the 1850s, the psychic fame of the Eddy family brought visitors from around the world. The small village of Chittenden, an old respectable farm community, soon became known as "The Spirit Capital of the World."

After Julia MacCombs married Zephaniah Eddy, the simple farmer discovered that his young wife had what was called "second sight." Her clairvoyance was so attuned that she could predict the future from the depths of a trance and hold conversations with spirits whose voices, she said, "were always talking away in my head."

Julia was not the first of her family to be possessed by spirits. It is recorded that her grandmother four times removed had been burned as a witch—or at least had been sentenced to that fate in the famous Salem trials of 1692.

Julia's children were born with similar spiritual abilities. The young boys, especially William and Horatio, were always falling into trances and speaking to invisible friends. Their father, convinced they were possessed by the devil, tried beating it out of them, but to no avail. Once, when he found William in a deep trance, Zephaniah summoned a neighbor, and together they poured a bucket of scalding water down William's back. But the boy didn't stir, though he carried the scars for the rest of his life.

The Eddy children were eventually banned from attending school because the knockings, levitating desks and voices from the beyond created chaos in the classroom.

By 1874, the boys had grown, and Zephaniah, weary from his farm work and his family's embarrassing notoriety, passed away. The remaining Eddy family converted part of the second floor of their farmhouse into a spiritual meeting place and began to hold séances every night of the week except Sunday. During the séances, spirits would not only communicate through voices, but would also make appearances for five-minute intervals. Sometimes the Eddy brothers would channel twenty to thirty spirits in one evening. It is recorded that some visitors traveled 3,000 miles in an attempt to contact a loved one who had passed away.

Eventually, as America's fascination with mediums died down, Chittenden went back slowly to being a quiet farming village. Horatio died in 1922 and William a decade later, at the age of ninety-nine.

A Chittendonian who used to take food to William during the last year of his life reports that the old medium rarely spoke—if anyone said anything, "it was usually William's dog"—but that he used to make his cane dance around the room.

Jonathan Koons

Around the same time as the Eddy boys were gaining fame for their ability to recall the dead, an Ohio farmer named Jonathan Koons discovered that he had an even more developed psychic tool. Koons found that if he put himself into a trance (similar to many of today's channelers) "ghosts" were able to communicate through him. Frequently, the spirits employed dialects and languages that Jonathan, an uneducated and unworldly man, had never heard before in his life. Uncanny as it sounds, it is also recorded that if a musical instrument was left unattended within Jonathan's trance range, it would suddenly burst into sound.

Koons's modest log house soon became well known as a place where seekers could meet with spirits. It became so celebrated that it was constantly crowded, although it was situated some 70 miles from the nearest town.

Although many investigations were held, the facts about Koons's abilities remained untouched by criticism. Eventually, however, Koons, persecuted by neighbors who did not appreciate his gift, was driven from his home and dropped out of sight.

Stainton Moses

Stainton Moses, born in 1839, was quite educated, unlike many mediums. After receiving a university degree from Exeter College, Oxford, he embarked on a career as both a clergyman and a schoolmaster.

In 1872, Stainton's life took a turn towards spiritualism. After attending a séance, he discovered that he himself possessed mediumistic gifts. Besides trance communication, he had a host of other psychic abilities including telekinesis, production of lights, perfumes, musical and rapping sounds and materialization of hands. Witnesses also reported that in his presence heavy tables would rise into the air and books and letters would float from one room to the next.

In 1882, as a result of his desire to unite intellectual reasoning with the religious implications of mediumship, Moses helped found the Society of Psychical Research in the United States, a group devoted to the investigation of paranormal phenomena. But only four years later, he resigned from the organization because of what he felt to be ill-treatment of mediums under investigation.

Edgar Cayce

By the narrowest definition, Edgar Cayce was neither a medium nor a channeler: While dictating messages, he always spoke in his own voice; no guides ever identified themselves as using Cayce's physical body; and when he communicated with the dead or with the minds of those living, the information appeared to emanate from Cayce's own subconscious. Unlike many contemporary channels, in touch with entities from several dimensions (past, future, interplanetary), Edgar Cayce was quite possibly in touch with the highest dimension—Universal Consciousness.

His contribution to our understanding of mediumship is impressive. According to records kept at the Association for Research and Enlightment in Virginia Beach, Virginia (a facility founded for the study of Edgar Cayce material), Cayce gave an estimated 16,000 psychic readings over the course of his lifetime. More than half of his readings dealt with imbalances concerning the mind and the physical body. There are also about 2,500 "Life Readings" based on the Akashic Records, or past lives.

Two-thirds of the readings were typed single-space and each one was approximately three-and-one-half pages in length. All in all, it is estimated that Edgar

Cayce dictated more than 12 million words. Almost as astounding is the fact that there was never an indication he was aware of even a single word he spoke. While in a self-induced trance state, Edgar Cayce may have made contact with the Cosmic Consciousness and gained knowledge that is limited neither by time nor space.

Born in 1877 on a farm near Hopkinsville, Kentucky, Edgar spent the early years of his life attending a local school. He was distracted most of the time and apparently learned very little. It's not surprising that his formal education ended after he completed the ninth grade. What is surprising is that despite his minimal education, while in a trance state Cayce displayed a profound knowledge of such sophisticated subjects as ancient languages, medicine, psychology and geology.

Edgar had his first psychic experience when he was only eight years old. While playing in the woods, he saw in a clearing a bright white light that spread across his entire vision. Out of the light a voice spoke: "Your prayers have been heard. What would you ask of me that I may give you?" The child was obviously not frightened by the light. His answer was thoughtful; some might say divine. He answered: "I'd like to be able to help other people, especially sick children—and to love my fellow men."

On the following day, Edgar was even more distracted than usual. He was barely able to sit through school, and in the evening he found it even harder to concentrate on his homework. By eleven at night, more exhausted and distraught than ever, Edgar was still trying to finish his studies. Suddenly, he heard the voice again, the same one he had spoken with in the woods. This time the voice said, not once but several times, in a chanting, calming manner: "Sleep, we will help you." Edgar followed the advice.

When he awoke early the next morning, he discovered that all the work he had struggled with the night before was now clearly and firmly placed in his mind.

Not too long after this experience, Cayce suffered an accident not uncommon among young boys: He was hit by a baseball. Left semiconscious from the injury, Edgar instructed his mother to put a compress of specific medicinal mixtures at the bottom of his skull. The next day, he was back to normal. It was as though he had never suffered the injury at all.

This was probably the first time Cayce had ever prescribed a healing instruction. However, when he was twenty-three, he was to call on his powers once again to heal himself. This time, however, word of his miraculous recovery spread throughout the medical community.

On the evening of April 18, 1900, Cayce was working as a salesman in the W. R. Bowles Photography Gallery. Suddenly, and for no apparent reason, he lost his voice. General practitioners as well as specialists tried treating Cayce, but to no avail. Finally, with the help of Dr. A. C. Layne, an osteopath, Cayce took his treatment into his own subconscious.

Dr. Layne (who was also a hypnotist) put Cayce to sleep and gave him the suggestion to have his subconscious mind look at his throat, diagnose the problem and find a remedy. While in a trance, Cayce diagnosed the problem as partial paralysis of his vocal cords caused by nerve strain. To correct it, his unconscious suggested that the flow of blood should be increased to the area for a short amount of time.

Layne then instructed Cayce to follow the suggestion and increase the blood flow to his vocal cords. As he did this, Layne reported that Cayce's neck turned

a deep red. When Layne then suggested the blood flow
should return to normal, the flush faded away. After
Cayce awoke, his voice was normal, but he had no
recollection of anything that had taken place while
he was in the trance. From the time of that incident,
a professional as well as personal relationship developed between Cayce and Layne.

On June 17, 1903, Gertrude Evans and Edgar Cayce
were married in Hopkinsville. Barely a week later,
Layne asked Cayce to help him diagnose one of his
patient's problems. Edgar agreed. With Layne's support, Cayce went into a trance to obtain the necessary
information on the illness; together they cured the
patient. During the following days, Cayce and Layne
diagnosed the illnesses of several other patients.

News of the team's ability to help solve medical
mysteries was reported in the Bowling Green newspaper, *The Times Journal,* on June 22, 1903:

IN A TRANCE BOWLING GREEN MAN IS ABLE TO DIAGNOSE
HUMAN ILLS. HAS NO RECOLLECTION OF IT WHEN HE
AWAKES, AND DOES NOT PRETEND TO UNDERSTAND HIS
WONDERFUL POWER.

Dr. A. C. Layne, osteopath and magnetic healer, was
in the city Sunday from Hopkinsville to have Edgar
Cayce diagnose a case for him. This sounds peculiar in
view of the fact that Mr. Cayce is not a physician and
knows nothing in the world about medicine or sur-
gery.

Since Mr. Cayce has been living in this city he lost
his voice and was unable to speak a word. He returned
to his former home in Hopkinsville and was there
treated by Dr. Layne and had his voice restored. At
this time it was discovered that Mr. Cayce possessed
unusual mediumistic powers and since then he had
discovered that by lying down, thoroughly relaxing
himself and taking a deep breath he can fall into a

trance, during which, though he is to all appearances asleep, his faculties are alert. Some time ago, Dr. Layne had him go into a trance and diagnose a difficult case at Hopkinsville.

The diagnosis proved to be correct in every particular and it was not long until the patient recovered.

The physicians had been unable to diagnose the case. Yesterday he came here to have Mr. Cayce diagnose another case and it was done in the presence of several people at Mr. Cayce's home on State Street.

The patient is not here, but is ill at his home in Hopkinsville. Cayce went into his trance and then the doctor told him that the patient's body would appear before him and he wanted him to thoroughly examine it from head to foot and tell him where the diseased parts were located.

In a moment more the doctor commenced at the head and asked Cayce minutely about every part of the body. He answered, telling of the location of blood clots, that one lung was sloughing off and detailed other evidences he saw of disease. It was as if the body was immediately before him and he could see through it and discern plainly every ligament, bone and nerve in it.

Dr. Layne was thoroughly satisfied with the diagnosis and when it was completed had Mr. Cayce diagnose several other cases of less importance and then left for his home and will base the treatment of each case on the diagnosis as given by Cayce.

Mr. Cayce does not know what he is saying while in the trance, nor when it is over has he any recollection of what he said. He does not pretend to understand it and is not a spiritualist in any sense of the word, but is an active member of the Christian Church.

After the birth of his son Hugh, though still working with doctors, Cayce pursued a career as a photographer and opened his own studio in Bowling Green.

Unfortunately, two devastating fires destroyed his business, forcing the family to return to Hopkinsville. But the Cayces' lives were never to be quiet again. Word of the "miracles" of Edgar Cayce was spreading to cities across the nation.

Stories reported that Cayce needed only to be given the name and address of a patient, wherever he or she was, and he was then able to tune in telepathically to that individual's mind and body as easily as if he or she were in the same room.

In his book *Venture Inward*, Hugh recalls how his father conducted his readings:

> Someone would request a reading by letter, telegram, phone or in person. An appointment would be set for 11 A.M. or 3 P.M. on a specified day. The applicant did not have to be present with my father. It was necessary that Edgar Cayce be given the real name and address where the person would be at the specified time. He could be anywhere in the world. Anyone could give the instructions and ask the questions. My mother was the "conductor" for most of them.
>
> At the appointed time Edgar Cayce would come in from his garden or from fishing, or from working in his office. He would loosen his tie, shoelaces, cuffs, and belt and lie down on a couch. His hands, palms up over his forehead, were later crossed over his abdomen. He would breathe deeply a few times. When his eyelids began to flutter, it was necessary to read to him a suggestion-formula which had been secured in a reading in answer to the request. It was also necessary to watch the eyelids carefully. If they were allowed to flicker too long before the suggestion was read, my father would not respond. He might then sleep for a couple of hours or more and awaken refreshed without knowing he hadn't given a reading.
>
> When the reading was concluded and Edgar Cayce would say, "We are through for the present," the con-

ductor would say . . . "Now perfectly normal, and perfectly balanced, you will wake up."[5]

Cayce's readings supported the concept that the mind is strongly connected to illness. "Mind is the builder" is a phrase he often repeated, especially when referring to cancer. Although his readings were given long before our current understanding of the growth of the disease, while in a trance he drew these conclusions: "Cancer is that which lives upon the cellular force by the growth itself. It is caused by breaking of tissue internally which is not covered sufficiently by the leukocyte due to the low vitality in the system."

Cayce did not make a conclusive statement about the relationship between cancer and heredity, though he did say that tendencies were most likely passed on and suggested that the family members of cancer victims should attempt to strengthen their own blood chemistry.

Cayce also regarded emotion as a strong contributor to illness. During one reading he warned, "Anger causes poisons to be secreted." Another time he said, "Keep the healthy mental attitude, never resentment, for this naturally creates in the system forces that are hard on the circulation, especially where there is some disturbance of the spleen and the pancreas. An attitude of resentment will produce inflammation." Cayce added, "Just as hate and animosity and hard sayings create poisons in the body, so do they weaken and wreck the mind of those who indulge in them."

Invalids from all over the country began to contact Cayce after reading these newspaper headlines from 1910–11 reporting his powers:

MARVEL DOCTOR DISCOVERED
ILLITERATE YOUTH IN HYPNOTIC CONDITION DOES

WONDERS, SAYS PHYSICIAN
                                    —*Boston Record Herald*

ILLITERATE MAN BECOMES A DOCTOR WHEN HYPNOTIZED
STRANGE POWER SHOWN BY EDGER CAYCE PUZZLES
    PHYSICIANS
                                    —*New York Times*

PSYCHIST DIAGNOSES AND CURES PATIENTS
IGNORANT OF MEDICINE, TURNS HEALER IN TRANCE
KENTUCKIAN NEW PUZZLE FOR PHYSICIANS
                                    —*Chicago Examiner*

In 1912, overwhelmed by the press's attention, Edgar decided to lead a quieter, less public life. He attempted to give up psychic readings and moved with his family to Selma, Alabama. There, he opened another photography business. But in 1914, he went back to Kentucky, to Lexington, to give a reading to one Mrs. Delaney, who had written saying she was paralyzed and desperate. After Cayce's reading, Delaney was cured and Cayce was back in the limelight. It was during this trip that Cayce met David Kahn, who would for many years remain a staunch advocate of his friend's gifts.

Kahn's interest was first sparked by the Delaney case and was fueled by his own early readings, when Cayce predicted the exact troop movements that he would soon experience during army duty in World War I.

When the war was over, Kahn arranged for another meeting with his friend. Cayce recommended that the young man leave his family's grocery business and enter into "wood and metal products." It was around this time that radios were first being developed, and would be placed in wooden cabinets in millions of American homes. In only a few years, David Kahn became a successful businessman, manufacturing and selling more radio cabinets than any other person in America.

In 1920, Edgar Cayce himself went in search of fortune. His motives, however, were in keeping with his nature: He wanted desperately to earn enough money to build a hospital dedicated to healing anyone in need. For three years, along with Kahn, he followed his dream, giving readings for oil drillers in Texas. Though his readings were often accurate, and though he traveled throughout the United States raising money for the project, his dream was not ready to materialize. Edgar returned to Selma, a financial failure.

In 1923, Arthur Lammers, a successful Ohio printer, came to Cayce for a reading. Lammers was so impressed he urged Cayce to give up his work as a photographer and devote himself completely to his psychic gifts. Lammers promised to fund an office for him in Dayton, Ohio.

Edgar moved once again with his family. From his Dayton office, Cayce began to give not only medical healing sessions but "Life Readings." He had no knowledge of Buddhism, Hinduism or Western metaphysics, yet when Cayce gave his Life Readings he would refer to "previous incarnations." When his words were first read back to him, Cayce was disturbed. A devout Christian, he was upset by the seemingly contradictory concepts of Heaven and Hell and repeated lifetimes.

It's understandable that Cayce would feel discomfort over the concept of reincarnation. Throughout his life, he maintained an active interest in Christianity. At an early age, in fact, he had even planned to become a preacher. (It wasn't unusual for the language of his readings to have a biblical flavor.) During his years in Hopkinsville, Louisville, Bowling Green and Selma, he was a Sunday School teacher and spent some part of every day reading the Bible, praying and meditating.

After his disturbing first Life Reading to Mr. Lammers, Cayce went back to the Bible for clarification and support. In rereading passages of the Old and New Testaments, he found mention of principles of Christianity that could support the theory of reincarnation and karma. Within the basic Christian tenet "As you sow, so shall you reap," Cayce felt there was an apt description of the concept of karma. His mind and heart at ease, he subsequently gave thousands of Life Readings.

The following are excerpts from a Life Reading given to a fourteen-year-old boy on August 29, 1927:

. . . to those experiences in the earth's plane and the urges seen from the sojourns, we find:

Before this the entity was in that period when the people in France were near to the rebellion, during the period of Louis XIII. The entity then was among those who were the escorts and protectors of that monarch; he was especially the one who chose the dress or the change of apparel for that ruler—though not in the capacity of the valet. Rather the entity was one who set the style for the people. The name then was Neil . . .

Before that we find the entity was in what is now known as Salonica, during the period when there were changes in the land. The entity was then among the tradespeople, in the name Cohal, and the entity gained and lost through that period—gaining in the service to country and to the people whom the entity served— losing in the application of self when the entity was put in power or position . . .

Before that we find the entity was in the land now known as Persia, when the people were divided in the service of the people who brought divisions in the land. Then the entity, as a physician in the court, gained and lost—or lost and gained. He lost through misapplication of himself to that for which the entity stood. He gained through the services rendered, even when persecutions came through the invading forces. The name was then Abiel . . .

Before that we find the entity was in the Egyptian land during the period when there was a division of the kingdom. The entity was among those people who were of the native folk, yet the one who brought much comfort to many people in providing for the application of truth which was given by those in rule—so that the native understood the intent and purpose. The entity acted then in the capacity of teacher, minister, or the go-between between the priests of the day and the common people. The name then is Isois . . .

Before that the entity was in the Atlantean land when the floods came and when destruction ruled in that land. The entity was among those so destroyed from that experience, being among the people in power and the successor to the throne, had that land remained. Gaining, and losing in that experience through the misapplication of self to the lessons or tenets which were in the way of being applied by the entity. The name was the Amiaieoulieb . . .[6]

Cayce continued an active practice of Life Readings and healing diagnosis in Dayton until Lammers's business fell into difficulty.

His old friend, David Kahn, was back to the rescue. Kahn gathered together several investors who agreed to contribute to the creation of a hospital and research facility in Virginia Beach, Virginia. The Cayce family moved from Dayton to Virginia Beach in 1925.

Within two years, the Association of National Investors was incorporated. Its purpose was not only to further encourage the benefits thousands were deriving from Cayce's personal readings and healings, but also to engage in general psychic research.

It looked for a while as though Edgar Cayce's dream was going to come true. But in April of 1929, he predicted the Wall Street crash. His prophecy was based on a dream that a broker had asked Cayce to decipher. He foresaw a wild panic in the money market—not only on Wall Street, but in other centers throughout the country and the world. Six months later, on October 29, 1929, the stock market crumbled. With the depression came the loss of the hospital. However, the research facility continued to exist, as did Cayce's healings and readings.

Clearly, Cayce had another remarkable gift—prophecy. In June of 1931 he was working in his garden. Suddenly, he dropped his hoe and rushed into the house. He locked himself in his study and came out hours later, distraught. He told his family that he had a vision of the approach of the Second World War, and that millions of men and women would perish.

During a reading on October 7, 1935, he made this statement on European political affairs:

As to affairs of an international nature, we find a condition of great anxiety on the part of many; not only of individuals but of nations. And activities already begun have now assumed such proportions that groups will attempt to attach penalties and set up groups to carry them out. This will cause a taking of sides, as it were, by various other groups, countries or governments. Such will be manifested by the Austrians and Germans and later on the Japanese joining this influence. Thus an unseen force, gradually growing, must result in an almost direct opposition to the Nazi, or Aryan, theme. This will gradually produce a growth of animosities. And unless there is interference

by which many call supernatural forces and influ-
ences—which are active in the affairs of nations and
peoples—the whole world, as it were, will be set on
fire by militaristic groups and people who are for
power and expansion.[7]

Cayce's predictions concerned not only political
events, but also the earth's environmental metamor-
phosis and its natural catastrophes. Over the years,
Cayce accurately predicted several earthquakes and
volcanic eruptions. He saw the years between 1958
and 1998 as a period of intense movement below the
earth's surface, and said, in a reading in 1936, that
"there [would] be a change in the physical aspect of
the West Coast of America."[8] He also predicted that
solar power would ultimately be far more important
to man than nuclear power.

Cayce was also able to foresee his own death. The
great psychic did not have the physical stamina needed
to support his constant channeling. In his unending
efforts to heal, share insights and forewarn, he continually overburdened his energy source.

In fact, doctors were not the only ones to warn him
to slow down: During several readings, his own subconscious told him that he was killing himself by
draining his energy with the numbers of readings he
was giving. Whether it was a neurotic compulsion or
the altruistic wish to honor the thousands of desperate
requests he received weekly from across the world
that drove him on, we'll never know. But Cayce refused to lighten his schedule.

He retreated to a nursing home in Roanoke, Virginia, but he wasn't able to find any peace there. He
returned home and on New Year's Day, 1945, he announced: "I am going to be healed on Friday, January

5." His family and friends were soon to learn the true nature of his predicted self-healing. On Friday, January 5, 1945, they attended his funeral.

Throughout his life, Edgar Cayce was keenly aware of the responsibility that accompanied his gift. He saw the importance of the balance that must exist between the commitment required of a genuine seeker and the dedication of a channeler:

> In seeking information there are certain factors in the experience of the seeker and in the channel through which such information may come. Desire on the part of the seeker to be shown. And, as an honest seeker, he will not be too gullible; neither will he be so encased in prejudices as to doubt that which is applicable in his experience. Hence the information must not only be practical but it must be rather in accord with the desires of the seeker also. . . .
> On the part of that channel through whom such information may come, there must be the unselfish desire to be of aid to a fellow man. Not as for self-exaltation because of being a channel. Not for self-glorification that such a channel may be well spoken of. But rather as one desirous of being a channel through which the highest spiritual forces may manifest in bringing to the material consciousness of the seeker those things that may be beneficial in a spiritual and material sense to the seeker. . . .
> The soul of the seeker is passive, while the soul of the individual through which information comes is positive. As the physical is subjugated into unconsciousness the latter goes out, guided by suggestion, on the forces which are released to that individual place of the seeker. And the souls commune with one another.[9]

Edgar Cayce's documents—over 14,000 stenographic records—have been microfilmed and are on file with the Library of Congress in Washington, D.C. In addition, his readings are available through the Association for Research and Enlightenment, which is maintained by the Edgar Cayce Foundation in Virginia Beach, Virginia.

Throughout the world, those who are interested in the investigation of psychic phenomena continue to study the incredible legacy left by Edgar Cayce.

Jane Roberts

LISTENING

I've put the glass of my mind
so close to the cosmic wall
that I've become addicted to the strange
sounds
and eternal rattlings,
as if a multitudinous mouse
went scurrying—
Is that all I'm hearing?

—Jane Roberts[10]

In 1963, at a time when mediumship was not at its most popular, Jane Roberts began to channel the entity Seth. Her psychic initiation began in September of that year. While Jane was writing poetry, she suddenly felt her consciousness leave her body. Her mind was filled with ideas that seemed to emanate from outside herself. When she went back inside her body, she discovered that she had written, in a script other than her own, an entire manifesto entitled "The Physical Universe as Idea Construction." Her words and thoughts, she assumed, were a result of automatic writing.

Spurred by her experience, Jane and her husband, Robert Butts, an artist and writer, began to experiment with the Ouija board in their Elmira, New York, home. Seth introduced himself to Jane and Robert one October evening by pointing messages out on the board and claiming to be an "energy personality essence" called Seth. He entered Jane's life when she was thirty-five.

On May 8, 1929, Jane was born into a poor and troubled family in Saratoga Springs, New York. Her mother, whom she never saw walk, was bedridden as a result of painful, crippling arthritis. She was an angry woman, bitter that her illness took away the one gift she valued most—her beauty. Her rage would sometimes erupt, and when it did it was directed at either Jane or her husband. By the time Jane was three years old, her parents had divorced and the family was forced to live on welfare.

As a child, Jane's grandfather assumed the role of the important male figure in her life. She identified strongly with the older man, who was of Canadian and Indian heritage. His close relationship to nature was appealing to the sensitive, often solitary young girl. Her grandfather and her mother were estranged because of an old family argument that separated them for twenty years. But Jane and her grandfather met often and went for long walks in the woods. As they stepped through brambles and over rocks, listening to the rush of waterfalls and the breezes murmuring through the trees, he would retell ancient Indian legends and talk about the spirit in wind and fire.

Even that escape from her unhappy existence was

to be taken away. When Jane was ten years old, her mother was so riddled by arthritis that she was unable to care for her daughter; for eighteen months, Jane lived in a Roman Catholic orphanage in Troy, New York. During her time in St. Vincent's Female Orphanage, her innate mystical nature (Jane believed that statues of Christ could move) was heightened by the religious teachings stressed there.

Jane found safety in religious dogma; it helped explain her own mystical experiences. She keenly identified with the miracles associated with the saints. Jane was so moved, she decided to become a nun. But when she shared her ambition with her parish priest, he discouraged her, saying that she was needed more by her mother than by the Church. It is more likely that, intuitively, he saw Jane's mysticism as unfitting to the organization of the Church.

Probably as a result of taking several different drugs to relieve her pain, Jane's mother's behavior became increasingly erratic after Jane returned home. She disdained her daughter's newfound religious and mystical enthusiasm. She also had fits of depression so severe that they led to several suicide attempts. In order to maintain love and acceptance by her mother, and to avoid provoking any further hateful and frightening outbursts, Jane began to channel her psychic energies into more acceptable directions: poetry and art. She abandoned all pursuit of psychic knowledge.

Jane attended Skidmore College on scholarship. She did well in subjects she enjoyed, especially English and art, but did rather poorly in other areas. She had boyfriends, but didn't share the dreams of her other classmates: She never thought about marriage, children or keeping house.

In 1950, on an impulse, she ran off with her boyfriend and traveled across the country with him on his motorcycle. Despite her ambivalence about marriage, Jane dared not return to Saratoga without a license. Her marriage lasted three years, during which time she held various jobs—as a teacher, editor, assistant director of an art gallery, door-to-door salesperson and department supervisor in a radio factory.

It wasn't until after her divorce, and her second marriage, this time to Robert Butts in 1954, that Jane began to focus her energies exclusively on writing and psychic development.

During her lifetime she published more than a dozen books, several written by herself, and several others as a channel for the words of Seth, most notably the Seth Speaks series. She also wrote works of fiction, poetry and children's literature. Her last two books, *From This Rich Bed*, an autobiography, and *Sumari Songs*, poems written while in a trance, were in progress when she died of a lingering illness on September 5, 1984.

In the beginning Jane and Robert were secretive about their encounters with Seth. One night, when Seth was communicating with them, a neighbor was alarmed when he overheard his loud, deep, oddly accented voice. The neighbor knocked on the Butts' door, wondering who their visitor was and whether the couple was in any danger. Robert said it was only the television, and the neighbor left, satisfied by the explanation.

But as Jane later remarked, their "excuse" wasn't that farfetched. Very often she felt as though she was tuning into another frequency of reality on the "Seth channel." Though many different "stations" (entities) were eventually to open up to her, Seth was her main channel—the "commentator," as she occasionally referred to him.

Jane was a confirmed night owl and felt certain senses weren't really awakened in her until the sun had set. It was on Wednesday and Friday evenings after 9:00 P.M. that she would allow Seth's presence to inhabit her physical form. At this time, she would simply alter her consciousness. Robert would take off Jane's glasses and then begin to write down Seth's dictations. It wasn't long before their house was filled with "students" interested in studying Seth's messages; sometimes as many as forty people would come to their ESP classes to hear the entity speak.

But once Jane and Robert began holding sessions with Seth in order to work on their book projects, they held them almost always without witnesses. Seth spoke on those occasions at a slow enough pace for Robert to be able to take down his words verbatim. (He found it more personal to write out Seth's comments rather than to use a tape recorder; it also enabled him to insert his own observations.)

"Rubert," as Seth liked to call Jane, once wrote an essay describing her relationship to Seth and how she experienced channeling his entity. The following is an excerpt:

> As Jane, I'm not discarded when I'm in such a trance. Yet I step out of my Jane-self in some indescribable way, and step right back into it, when the session is over. So there must be another "I" who leaves Jane patiently waiting at the shore while "I" dive headlong into those other dimensions of experience and identity. Once the almost instant transformation is over, "I" become Seth or Seth becomes what I am. And in that state, the conditions of perception are those native to other lands of consciousness than ours.
>
> Such sessions never wear me out. Instead, I'm more refreshed than I was earlier. Usually I have little idea of time. As Seth I may speak for an hour, but when I

"snap back" I'll look at the clock in surprise, thinking
that fifteen minutes have passed at most. . . .

The trance state is characterized by a feeling of
inexhaustible energy, emotional wholeness, and sub-
jective freedom.[11]

Unlike Edgar Cayce, who would go into a sleep trance
and never remember a single word of his transmission, Jane Roberts was conscious during the Seth sessions and could often recall fragments of the entity's
message as well as her own physical placement during
the readings. She was *never* asleep at those times.

It is indisputable that Jane's day-to-day consciousness was altered by her experiences with Seth. One
sunny afternoon while sitting in the car waiting for
her husband to finish some chores at a local store, she
experienced a definite shift in her consciousness. The
world had changed. Everything was different, yet
everything was the same. The world sparkled. Every
blade of grass, every shopping cart glistened with a
crystalline energy. Each object, each person, was distinct and separate, but sang with a new sense of
uniqueness and perfection. Their individual places in
the universe all seemed *absolutely* necessary and in-
tegrated, but also remarkably isolated.

A sharp, extremely pleasant and exciting duality
had suddenly come into focus. It was as though Jane
had changed the lenses in her glasses to achieve a
super-clear multidimensional vision. Every object and
every person appeared to be a prototype from another
time, with their present existence inspired from the
original forms. We can perhaps get a better sense of
that glowing shift in her reality from her own words:

This particular scene with cars parked and others
pulling in and out is all imbued with a greatness in it-

self, yet the scene exists beyond itself at the same
time. I actually see this extra reality over the reality
we know, so everything in my view *is* super-real and
each person's reality is obviously and clearly more
than three-dimensional . . .

It's as if all the people I see are versions of the same
people, say, that were painted centuries ago by the old
masters; new versions, yet unique variations of themselves, their own originality altering the models even
while their existence rises from them.[12]

Experiences such as these, which occurred outside
her trance state, were fairly common for Jane. As a
result, she gained an illuminating understanding of
her reality and its relationship to reincarnation. (She
developed her ideas about reincarnation in *Psychic
Politics* and *Adventures in Consciousness*.) Jane saw
past, present and future lives as stemming from a
"source self." Our present she described as being focused on our physical reality. Personalities that were
reincarnated were different focuses that existed in some
way in a three-dimensional experience. But all personalities came from the original source self.

With this theory in mind, Jane felt that we could
gain a glimpse into our past lives when any focus
personality left its usual perceptual devices. By altering the direction of our awareness, we could enable
our present selves to open onto the screen of other
dimensions. Indeed, her husband experienced many
such reincarnational flashbacks. Rob's first experience took place on the afternoon of October 27, 1974.
Around 5:00 P.M., Rob had a vision of himself on a
Roman warship around the first century A.D. He per-
ceived himself as a large man with a big chest and
thick arms and legs. (In his present life, Rob is slim
and delicate.) He saw himself wearing a Roman uni-

form—short skirt, a vest decorated with circular med-als and a heavy metal helmet.

In another vision, again with himself as the Roman captain, he saw another man on board the ancient ship who he *knew* was, in his present life, Tam Moss-man, editor of the Seth books at Prentice-Hall. (Moss-man is now a channel for an entity named James, and edits a newsletter devoted to channeling.) Jane Rob-erts explained her husband's Roman captain as focus personality, existing in another time and place, though Rob himself exists in our current reality.

Roberts saw life and death as doors that lead us through our three-dimensional lives. Without death, we might otherwise be set in only one "time-and-space slot." The entity Seth also dealt often with the subject of past lives. When a minister asked Roberts, while she was channeling Seth, what determines the Bardo length (time lapses between our incarnations), Seth responded:

> You. If you are very tired, then you rest. If you are wise, you take time to digest your knowledge and plan your next life, even as a writer plans his next book. If you have too many ties with this reality or if you are too impatient, or if you have not learned sufficiently, then you may return too quickly. It is always up to the individual. There is no predestination. The answers are within yourself then, as the answers are within you now.[13]

Often it was difficult for Roberts, as well as her readers, to be able to decipher where she stopped and Seth began, or where less prominent entities entered. One of her critics, Charles H. Hapgood, a scientific writer and expert on Elwood Babbitt, stated: "It is possible for them [Jane and her husband] to limit to some degree Seth's expression by the questions they ask him and by the finite ideas he sees in their minds and must address himself to. He has to reach them at their level of understanding, which is a highly intellectualized one."

Jane continually questioned the element of inspiration and introspection, versus entity influence. She admitted that she could be smoking, drinking coffee, even listening to rock music when she would be aware that one part of her consciousness was coming into contact with a "particular station" and to some degree merging with it. "It's like sitting at the threshold of yourself," she explained.

In order for Jane Roberts to be able to accept the influence of another dimension, she had to put her ego aside and allow her intuition to open up, unheeded by interference. Her intellect, or mind, was "passive, yet poised." Sometimes she would feel her physical body become drowsy and would have to refocus her energy in order to stay balanced and not fall into a state of complete trance. During these delicate balances, Roberts wrote material *not* dictated by Seth.

During her communication with Seth, when Roberts would enter a trance state, her personality focus would blur and step aside *completely* to allow Seth to utilize her as a medium. She would not be involved in any other activities that might interfere with her reception. During the Seth Trance, the "I" of Jane would turn into what Seth is. "I am aware of being inside what he is," Roberts wrote, "to some extent basking in his exuberance, energy, and wisdom. In one way or another, Seth comes into my home station. Whatever his reality elsewhere, during a session he is 'alive' and immediate."[14]

Others might have been fearful of continual "intrusions" by entities, but Roberts had complete confidence that the universe was benevolent. She did not believe in good or bad spirits, in demon possession or evit intent. This may be one of the reasons she was such a ready and open medium. It also helped her to guide others away from drowning in a well of fear when, unprepared, they experienced certain kinds of phenomena.

When a young woman once telephoned Jane to tell her that she was "hearing voices," Roberts was not in the least bit hesitant to explore the nature of the voices. The woman described one voice, emanating from her head, as that of "God," and another voice, that of her dead father, emanating from her belly. The caller was quite distraught. She had just finished reading a book on possession, and was now certain that demons had begun to inhabit her body even though, she explained, she also had a "guide" voice that was trying to help her.

No doubt, members of the psychological community would have a heyday with this woman. Most likely she would be labeled a schizophrenic, and would be drugged, perhaps hospitalized.

When the woman told Jane she was trying to get the voices to go away but they wouldn't obey, Jane responded by explaining that she was dealing with her problem in the wrong way, making things more difficult for herself. Jane's interpretation may sound like psychological jargon, but the depth of her understanding is remarkable. She explained:

> . . . The voices represent aspects of yourself that you're inhibiting. So they do have messages that are important. They aren't alien—just part of your thought processes that you've denied. They become segmented. One voice represents the doubts that you aren't expressing, that you ignore or try to deny. The guide

voice represents an idealization of the self you want to
be. . . . As I listen to you, it's obvious that the guide
voice is setting up a superhuman pattern of behavior
that no person could achieve.[15]

Roberts felt that the distressed woman's conven-
tionalized beliefs about good and evil were causing
her to misunderstand the guide aspect of her personality. Since the woman only permitted herself to read
inspirational and religious literature, she had subconsciously closed down any outlet for her doubting
self. When her repressed doubts rose to the surface,
Roberts felt the woman translated them into evil forces
rather than seeing them as unofficial voices clamoring
for her attention.

Psychological healing was particularly fascinating
for Roberts, but she explored certain dimensions of
physical disease as well. Jane saw illness as emanating from the blockage of energy caused by linear consciousness. If reality was viewed narrowly, she believed
that certain assumptions were fed that eventually led
to contradictions, fears—and finally, disease. She was
so concerned with the relationship of emotional health
to physical well-being that during one of her semi-
trance states, she outlined over a dozen chapters for
a proposed book (never written) entitled *The Way Toward Health*.

She believed it was superficial to look at disease as
though it were something that came from outside in-
fluences. Instead, she felt that illness developed from
our own inner beliefs and desires: "Until we realize
that our consciousness, working through the body,
creates its state of being, then any natural cures will
be considered miraculous." On this topic, Seth explained: "So-called miraculous cures are simply ex-
amples of unimpeded nature." (Here we have a good

example of the convergence of Seth/Mind with Roberts/Mind.)

Again, the conclusions drawn by Seth and by Roberts are similar on the subject of creativity. Seth told Roberts during one session, "To some degree, creativity always involves a *denial* of life's daily official evidence, for creativity deals with that which you are about to bring into being. You are quite aware of the absence which you intend to fill. This applies obviously in the case of invention. Creativity involves productive change." On the following day, Jane Roberts wrote these notes:

> The world is our mental invention. Maybe that's been the real 'secret' all along and the one main issue that we've never understood. The natural world isn't our invention alone, of course. We share the creative venture with all of the other species. But the social, economic, artistic, political world—that *is* our exclusive invention. . . .
>
> Of course we must pay attention to the evidence of our senses, but when we begin to use our imaginations we bring a different knack into play—that of creating a divergent picture of the world, adding new data that wasn't there before.[16]

Roberts's interest in the creative process reveals itself in most of her own works as well as those channeled by Seth. However, unlike many other of her publications, which won only the attention of occult enthusiasts, *The World View of Paul Cézanne: A Psychic Interpretation* received the respect of the art community, a highly unusual feat since Roberts claimed the book was written by Cézanne himself. Throughout the book Cézanne generously offers valuable technical information on color, form, portrait painting and aesthetics.

Within the body of the text Roberts (or Cézanne) explained in depth the artistic processes involved in painting. In one section, she discussed the use of brushstrokes. They give a painting an "overlife" and "vitality that is somehow apart from the painting's observable qualities . . . soaked in the very growing qualities of nature itself."

She also suggested that the artist must rely almost completely on the visual sense, and not utilize any sensations reached by use of the mind or any of the other senses: "The eye is innocent. Visual data thus reveals artistic truths that may otherwise escape us."

The medium's book of the dead master's advice was enthralling enough to receive a review in *American Artist*, a conservative journal. It read in part:

> This book is so unusual, so astounding, and so fertile in its ideas and their implications for the artist that, even if you choose not to read it, you should at least be aware that it exists.
>
> Whether or not these ideas are actually Cézanne's, as expressed through medium Jane Roberts (and I confess entertaining the notion that they might be), is really irrelevant. What is important is that these perceptive opinions about painting and viewing the world (or nature) are obviously those of an experienced and highly intelligent artist with something exciting and relevant to say.[17]

Roberts's intricate web of insights extended into diverse areas, weaving patterns that connected our material understanding with metaphysical dimensions. The power of pyramids was just one of the areas of metaphysical research that she—and Seth—explored.

During one session when Roberts was channeling Seth, two of her students reported that they saw a pyramid above the medium's head. It vanished when she came out of the trance. This event opened Jane's mind to the potency of the pyramid. The next time she channeled Seth, she actually felt the pyramid above her head, "not physical but just as real. I could feel my consciousness rushing upward, seeping out gradually at first, then faster." It wasn't long before Seth encouraged Jane and the group to utilize the image of the pyramid as a tool for expanding their consciousness:

> Concentrate on the feeling in the back of your skull. The feeling itself is the important thing, for from it the pyramid shape will form. The pyramid may appear differently to each of you, because it is your own personal path into probable realities. It may appear as a path or as a ray of light or in some form, but follow it with full confidence and freedom. Use my voice simply as a thread to accompany you, but concentrate upon your own feelings and sensations.[18]

From those instructions, Jane and her students visualized different phenomena from "a man who went into Nothing . . . split the side of Nothing . . . and saw the physical universe" to a "group of miniature people dancing in a circle, symbolizing energy."

The concepts of energy and light are threads that ran through *all* the Roberts and Seth materials. An especially vivid vision that Jane experienced occurred one night while she was sitting in her kitchen: An unmoving ball of golden light appeared alongside her refrigerator. It was waist-high and flat. Roberts was so startled she fell backwards and the light vanished instantly. She knew it was neither a hallucination nor a dream; she felt it was an event from another reality that symbolically represented "the light that unites both [Seth's and Roberts's] worlds."

Roberts maintained that *everything* was energy. She coined the psyche "awareized energy" and explained it as constantly creating a psychic pattern that determines the route of our lives. Seth described himself as an "energy essence personality." Roberts explained, "We create events naturally, in the same way that the earth produces trees, grain, . . . There is also an inner landscape of the mind that produces thought, experiences, events and dreams."

Jane saw the experience and interpretation of dreams as a key to understanding ourselves and the cosmos. She stressed the importance in the dream state of encounters with the dead, numerical symbolism and precognitions. During one session when Jane felt she was channeling the spirit of Carl Jung or his equivalent, she spoke precisely on the meaning of numbers in dreams.

Based on the correlations between emotions and the numerology of the soul, it was explained to her by Jung's spirit that often in dreams numbers may appear as words (1 as "one" or 4 as "for"), as well as symbolizing many other complex connections. Speaking through Jane, Jung gave the example of the number 5: "It can represent the birth of a new instability in the personality when it appears in dreams, for it represents an overswelling of the male or female element."

Although events in our dream state are experienced quite differently from events in our waking hours, Roberts contends that dream experience is just as *real* as daily life. Dreams also have, she believed, the ability to predict possible future events. But as a result of our limitations in interpreting our dreams, very often their precognitive clues are either overlooked or forgotten. "Doubtlessly," said Roberts, "future memories go unrecognized for this reason, but it's possible that with a change of attitude we could handle pre-cognition as easily as we handle ordinary memories."

Jane Roberts's scope as a medium ranged from the concrete to the conceptual. She made her followers *think*, offering information as diverse as an analysis of quantum mechanics to the meaning behind the migration of geese. But there's a shadow over her credibility. There are critics who maintain that Jane's personality actually created the Seth phenomenon, others who feel that Seth was ever-present in Jane's daily life. These are difficult points to argue since Jane admitted her trance state was usually not deep enough to obscure her memory, nor even her ego. Jane's extraordinary experiences in her waking state also seem to account for a kind of "bleed-through" of psychic phenomena. Perhaps it's most fruitful to listen to Jane's own opinion about her gifts:

> . . . it goes without saying that I make no "supernatural" claims. I don't materialize holy ash, or perform miracles at mid-day. I don't claim to be a healer, though I do believe that each of us has the ability to heal ourselves, and that some people are uniquely equipped to do so. I *do* proclaim the uniqueness of my own personality and its private connection with the universe, but I also maintain that each other individual is also unique with his or her own connection to the universe.[19]

Part
TWO

The Channelers
and
Their Entities

In order to accept channeling as an authentic phenomenon, or channelers as genuine vehicles for transmission of spirit, one must allow the cocoon of rigid beliefs and fear to be unraveled and the butterfly of spirit to be set free. At this moment the journey begins. Once the butterfly spreads its wings in joyous flight, the landscapes of other dimensions appear with their boundless and eternal messages of beauty and love.

Thousands of people from all walks of life, all areas of the country, have taken flight, experiencing this cosmic communication. Even more startling than the mass communion is the fact that the messages are all the same and appear to echo from a central "mountain" of higher or more evolved thought. It is as if there is a frequency—aptly characterized a "channel"—spreading through the waves of consciousness, telling us what perhaps we all once knew: We are the designers of our realities, *we* are responsible for our lives, limited only by our fears, a part of the Whole, the All, the Universal Oneness.

After speaking with hundreds of channelers across the country, I am left with more questions now than before my project began. Are there truly "guides" from other dimensions responsible for individual enlightment? Are the channelers themselves in touch with their own higher self, a deeper subconscious than even Freud or Jung imagined? Do they possess a stunning recall of the place from where they came and where we all will return? Could they in fact be receiving on a different vibrational level "postcards from home"? The Land of Light and Love. In the final analysis, where and from whom the messages emanate matters little. It is the *message* that is important—and it is important that we hear it.

I have attempted in the following pages to profile the leading channelers in the major cities of the United

States. In doing so, I have also tried, whenever possible, not to judge their particular gifts. All who are
represented are, I believe, sincere; some perhaps are
more evolved. The final assessment I leave to the reader.

Jach Pursel/Lazaris

My interview with Lazaris introduces this section of the book. Jach Pursel has been trance-channeling Lazaris, "The Consummate Friend," for over fifteen years. Currently, he is one of the most celebrated channels, and his video and audio tapes as well as his seminars are responsible for encouraging hundreds of individuals to develop their own channeling abilities.

ROBIN WESTEN: *There are so many people channeling and so many spirits or entities who are communicating. First of all, why? There have been channeling experiences throughout history, but why so many now?*

There are a number of reasons why there are so many beings who are channeling information. To appropriately answer, however, we must divide the group into two groups. There are the legitimate channels and the entities who come through them, and then there are those who, shall we say, are not legitimate.

The legitimate channeling experience has increased because people are ready to reach and stretch to new dimensions of their awareness. So many of you have looked—really looked—for the answers.

Sometimes you are not even sure of the questions

to ask, but you want the answers. You know that there is something more to life than just surviving, that there is something more than just acquiring, that there is something more than blind faith and empty hope. You know there is *something more*. You don't always know how to put the question, but you do know you want the answers. Your desire for answers has brought those who can help you find answers—not *the* answers but *your* answers.

More and more people from a vast variety of backgrounds are realizing that what is missing from their lives is a real sense of spirituality. In search of that spirituality, some are turning to the more fundamental and traditional sources—witness the increase in church activity. Others are looking for a new spirituality. They are truly ready for *something more*.

We like to say that we are here because we have been invited, both by the individuals with whom we work and by the humanity that we want to help you understand. We have been invited, and thus we respond. Those who are legitimate, we would imagine, feel the same way.

As far as the not-legitimate, their reasons for channeling what may, or may not, be an entity are as varied as they are. Often they are what we call the "bandwagoneers." They see what they deem a "good thing," and they see the seekers as "easy marks." So they jump on the bandwagon of the New Age. Some are deluded by their negative egos. Others are quite aware of their chicanery. It is sad.

RW: *Well, then, who are some of the good channels, and who are not?*

To answer that would not be appropriate. First, throughout the history of metaphysics and spirituality there have been the valuable and the not-so-valuable. Within traditional religion there are those who legitimately "receive the calling" and those who fake it. Within this new spirituality it is no different. Each must decide for themselves. That is part of the process.

Secondly, one of the lessons you have chosen to learn is to discern. Since discernment is a gift, use it.

Within the channeling field there is a broad range of participants. At one end there is charlatanism and chicanery. The middle range includes those with good intentions, but little contact, to those who have a strong contact but little insight. Then there are those who are channeling powerful energies with wonderful insights. You must decide from whom you wish to learn. Each of these groups has something to teach—it may not be something you want or need to learn. Sometimes it is best just to say, "I pass!"

Though you can learn from any of these participants, we suggest: Use discernment.

RW: *That makes sense. We each have to decide for ourselves. We each have to be responsible then. Lazaris, are there guidelines we could use to sort out who's worth listening to and who's not? What guidelines do you recommend we use when we discern?*

Definitely so! There are seven distinct criteria to use in determining if a source of channeled material is valuable or not. These, by the way, are the criteria we encourage people to use when they talk with us as well. You see, we do not want people coming to listen to us and believing everything we say just because "Lazaris said so." No! Take what we say and evaluate it. If it works, use it. If it doesn't work, let's talk. Perhaps you misunderstood or perhaps you could learn better from some other energy.

1. Consistency of the message. Is what the entity says consistent with what they have said before?

People can be inconsistent, but a valuable entity should not be. You see, as people you exist inside time and space, and therefore things happen linearly for you. What you thought was true last year or last week may be proved untrue today or tomorrow. Therefore, the unfolding of time/space allows for human inconsistency.

An entity exists outside of time/space. Your past, present, and future should be simultaneous to them, and their philosophical message should reflect that simultaneity by being consistent.

Messages about how you create your own reality, followed up by messages telling you something is inevitable and cannot be changed, betray inconsistency. Telling you, on the one hand, that you are God and that you are perfect just the way you are, and then telling you that you are so evil or so negative that the world has to be totally destroyed to purge itself of the harm, damage, or imperfection that you have done is inconsistent.

Your world is a world of possibilities and probabilities. Be wary of inevitabilities.

Understand that the message—the teachings—can build over time, but they should not be inconsistent with what was said before. If you find the inconsistencies, we are not saying you should run away—just walk more slowly and carefully.

2. Consistency of the personality. Is the mood and personality of the entity consistent and stable regardless of the mood of the channel? What you create happening in the world around you has impact on the mood you are in. Because you have space and time, those moods and your personality are going to shift—

hopefully a great deal in the positive direction and only slightly in the negative direction.

An entity, on the other hand, exists outside of time and space. Therefore moodiness and personality changes suggest that perhaps the entity is not as "otherworldly" as he or she claims to be.

By the way, that personality that is consistent should also be a pleasant one. That an entity is consistently rude and nasty or mean and hostile still is not a good sign. Put simply, an enlightened being just would not have an unpleasant personality.

3. Limited or unlimited message. Regardless of whether the information is psychic, philosophical, or a combination of both, it should be open and aiming toward creating a better reality. An unlimited message does not always just say, "Yes!" An unlimited message does not just deliver good news.

An unlimited message offers what we call "growth choices" rather than "fear choices." Even if the information isn't what you want to hear, it is information that can help you become more of who you are and more of who you are becoming.

If the message is limited and filled with fear choices, be wary.

4. Who has the power? The entities worth listening to are telling you and teaching you to take back your own power. Who has the power?

We would encourage you to be suspect of those who take power or who offer power-taking messages. Be alert to information that tells you that the entity is the only one who can help you or is the only one who can intervene on your behalf. Some who claim enlightment actually tell clients that "the only way Home" is through them and their teachings.

Others who claim some spiritual authority have

declared that they—the entity—would send solutions and gifts rather than teach the person how to create their own solutions and create their own gifts. Some entities have even used this supposed power to threaten people who considered "leaving the fold."

Further, you must look beyond the rhetoric. The proper words can be there, but what are the meaning and the actions that lie behind those words? It is one thing for an entity to tell you that you create your own reality. It is quite another for them to also show you and teach you how.

The alternative to "power-taking" is "power-restoring"—not "power-giving." Power is restored when you not only understand that you do create it all, but you also understand why and how you do it!

5. Positive or negative philosophy. Entities of value will have a positive philosophy. Their philosophy will see the hope and the possibilities of what humankind can be and can become. The teachings will be more than uplifting and inspiring; the goals will be reachable—they will be "be-able" and "do-able."

Psychic information may not always be positive, that is true. However, negative information will be discussed lovingly and will be accompanied by positive solutions. We state it again: Your world is a world of shimmering possibilities and probabilities. As possibilities become probabilities, you then choose the actualities. Nothing is inevitable. Nothing except the Love of God/Goddess/All That Is.

6. Check your feelings. If you have been listening to an entity of calibre, you will feel uplifted, inspired, hopeful, and confident in *your* abilities—grateful for theirs. When the interaction is over, how do you feel?

7. Does it work? "By your fruits . . ." The information you receive may sound wonderful, but does it

make sense and does it work in your life? If so, hurrah! If not, gently walk away.

RW: *I have heard many entities talk of God. God seems to be a very important part of this New Age. However, I hear you talking about God/Goddess/All That Is. Why do you use this particular term?*

. . . the concept of God is vitally important to the New Age. The term has been bandied about so much by so many people that the meaning has been lost. Others have used the term "New Age" as their chic jargon for so long that the meaning has evaporated. The New Age is, among other things, a new spirituality.

Spirituality is a loaded term. From earliest childhood memories you have ideas—you have pictures in your head—about what spirituality is. Often those ideas or pictures are scary or boring. Sometimes they are fanciful.

Spirituality is your relationship with God. The most devout Fundamentalists have a particular kind of relationship with God, but they do have a relationship and therefore they have a spirituality. The most determined agnostic also has a relationship with God and thus has a spirituality. The atheist, similarly, has a spirituality. Though he/she denies God, ironically, that denial constitutes a more active relationship than the indifference of many who habitually attend church on Sunday. Even the atheist is spiritual. Everyone, whether they want to admit it or not, is spiritual, because everyone has a relationship with God.

Now, as we were saying, the New Age is about developing a new relationship with God. Yes, God is a very important part of this New Age.

Part of developing that new relationship is to re-place inaccurate or only partially accurate ideas—old pictures—of God with more correct images. Everyone uses the word "God," but what does it mean? Obviously it is not a proper name—it's not a person.

God is the name given to the creator of all reality or the source—or Source (capital "S"), to be more respectful. God is All That Is.

Throughout the history of humankind, you have been looking to describe this Force in your attempts to get closer to It.

It has been called a number of Hebrew names. Each religion throughout the world has its many names for God. Additionally, God has been referred to as "The All," "Is-ness," "All-ness," "The God Force," "The God Energy." The list is probably endless.

For about 3,000 years the concept of God has been dominated by male chauvinism. God is seen as a man—preferably old, with a long white beard and definitely Caucasian! Prior to roughly 3,000 years ago, the pictures of God changed periodically from singular male and female faces to many faces, both female and male.

Many feminists are now saying that God is a woman and they are calling her Goddess. Some among them are encouraging a competitive stance between God and Goddess. They are arguing about who is better—who is more powerful. There are those who have taken all the stock phrases with the word "God" and re-placed them with the word "Goddess."

"Oh my Goddess, what happened? . . . Well, God-dess bless you! . . . May Goddess be with you . . . In Goddess's name . . ."

We would suggest that such behavior is just evidence of how pervasive male chauvinism really is in your world. The Goddess does not have to compete with God, just as women should not measure themselves by strictly male standards. Such a competitive stance suggests that those particular standards are better. They are not. The Goddess is powerful enough to stand on Her own.

The Source is not a man or woman, yet It is comprised of the energy of both. We would suggest that the Source is a synergy (the whole is greater than the sum of its parts) of all that is maleness and all that is femaleness.

Another way of saying this: The Source is not only the sum of all masculine energy and all feminine energy, It is an undefinable, indescribable, exponential *more*. The Source is God and Goddess and something that is more than either or both. It is All That Is.

Therefore, we refer not just to God or Goddess, though we honor both. We refer to God/Goddess/All That Is.

It is a mouthful, we realize. It is perhaps easier to refer just to God and placate yourself with a "Well, you know what I mean." The problem: We may know what you mean, but do *you*? Does your subconscious? Every time you reference God/Goddess/All That Is, you are supporting yourself with a new and much more correct image, picture, idea of the Source.

Besides, many people involved in this New Age—this New Spirituality—were at least passingly familiar with the popularity of Eastern thought in the West. If they were once willing to be a devotee of "Swami Sri Such-a-banana-bandanna-roseanna," certainly they can reach out to at least begin a relationship with God/Goddess/All That Is!

RW: *Lazaris, a common message in the New Age is that each of us creates our own reality. A common criticism is that such an attitude is socially and politically irresponsible. What do you say?*

Where to begin? As with any movement or field of study, in the field of metaphysics and the New Spirituality, there are those who know what they are talking about, and there are those who don't. Sometimes those who speak first, loudest, and most controversially are not the ones who necessarily know what they are talking about.

RW: *Could you explain that more fully?*

By looking at an entirely different field, perhaps we can make our point. Who spoke the loudest and was the most controversial about how to solve the social and economic problems in post–World War I? It was Adolf Hitler. Who spoke first, loudest, and most controversially about the concern of Communist infiltration of the United States after World War II? It was Joseph McCarthy.

We are not suggesting that anyone in the New Age or who is involved in channeling is like either of these two. No, they were archetypal, indeed. Our point is that sometimes those who speak the loudest are not correct in what they say.

Further, the media are looking for a story, which most often means controversy. It is understandable; they have to report what is going to sell advertising to stay in business.

To report how this New Age thought isn't really that bizarre—that it is an expansion of previous ideas, not a criticism or an attack—is, quite frankly, boring. It does not sell newspapers.

However, do a report on some outlandish half-truth about the New Age that is flamboyantly and almost tauntingly presented by a loud and controversial spokesperson—now *that* sells papers!

RW: *Please continue.*

All right. You create your own reality. In the Old Age of Metaphysics, this creation occurred in your subconscious or unconscious mind. In the New Age of Metaphysics and Spirituality, this creation occurs in the conscious mind.

The New Age, contrary to popular myth, is not a date. It is a state of mind. People have been discovering their New Age for thousands of years. And they will continue to discover it for thousands of years to come. It is just that many, many more are making that personal discovery *now*.

You enter your personal New Age when you are ready to know that you not only create your own reality, but that you do it consciously. Before you are ready to know that the creation is conscious, you are still in the Old Age. That is not bad or wrong—it just is.

That you do create your own reality is more than a philosophy. Your quantum physicists are consistently demonstrating in their scientific laboratories that reality is whatever your consciousness observes it to be. There are many differing theories, but they all agree Reality is not absolute, it is a product of thought and expectation. It is a product of expectation!

Ask even science buffs about the importance of "double blind" experiments, and without a blink of the eye they will tell you that the experimenter's expectation can color the results of an experience. Without missing a beat they will tell you that an experiment without the use of "double blind" procedures is discredited and invalid.

That is how powerful expectations and thoughts are. The basis of quantum science is that there is no such thing as an observer. Everyone is a participant.

RW: *Then you are saying that regardless of whether it is socially and politically irresponsible, it is true. We each do create our own reality.*

Exactly! You do, whether you want to believe it or not. You do create your own reality. Mystics have been telling you that for centuries, and now your own scientists, ironically, are proving it.

Just as they are proving what the Old Age Mystics have been saying, the New Age Mystics are now saying, "Yes, you do create your reality, and that creation is conscious."

RW: *But what about the responsibility issue?*

Again, those spokespersons who don't really know what the New Age of Spirituality is all about—or even know that much about the Old Age of Metaphysics, for that matter—often do talk and act irresponsibly. Just as some religious leaders and politicians—charged with overseeing the moral, social, and political responsibilities—talk and act irresponsibly.

The critics and detractors of the New Age say that such a philosophy is irresponsible because it eliminates social and political caring. The critics charge that a person who believes in this self-created reality idea will stop caring about hunger, poverty, and other human injustice. The detractors assume that the New Age seekers will turn their backs on all tragedy, saying, "Oh, well, they created that reality. It's none of my concern."

RW: *Yes, exactly.*

First, the critic is partially right. There are those who would say exactly that. It is sad. There are those who are very shallow and who are very non-caring and will use metaphysics and the New Spirituality as an excuse—as a place to hide. If they did not use the banner of the New Age to hide behind, they would find another excuse.

Then there are those who just do not know any better. They have learned surface metaphysics. They have learned jargon. These may be the well-intentioned, but they are looking for the simplest answers, and they settle for platitudes and clichés. Because they have not investigated the real meaning—because they have not looked at the depth of the metaphysics they teach or pretend to believe—they end up correctly accused by the critics and detractors. They *are* irresponsible.

The seekers who are sincere and who bother to look honestly at the philosophy by which they attempt to live will come to understand that they do create their whole reality. They create it by either causing it or by allowing it to happen.

Yes, those who are suffering tragically did create the reality, but so did the one who witnesses—directly or indirectly—that human injustice.

That you are aware of the problem means that you directly or indirectly created it by causing or allowing it to exist. No, we are not suggesting that you should feel guilty; we are saying that on some level you are responsible.

At this point some may wonder how they could, or why they would, create such tragedy for other people. Some may be saying, "I wouldn't create starvation for me, and I certainly would not for others." We are not saying you are creating the starvation by cause. We are saying you are allowing it to exist in the world.

Why? Well, some may be creating it to feel better than and superior to all those "less fortunate people."

Some may be creating the tragedy so they can play "savior." After all, if you are going to be a "knight in shining armor" you need either "a damsel in distress" or "firebreathing dragons" or both.

Some allow a world of tragedy so they can have a job trying to fix the world. Yet others allow such tragedy out of fear and doubt. Others have been taught that "that's just the way it is." They have been taught that by family, society, religion, and by peers. Perhaps they were taught by the very critics and detractors who say it is irresponsible to think you create it all!

The New Age seekers, who really understand what it means to create their own reality are, contrary to what the critics say, being very responsible. They know that the world "out there" will not change until they change "in here." And they know that the only way it will change "out there" is if it changes "in here."

There are no observers. Everyone is a participant.

Additional criticism: These New Agers will say of the less fortunate, "They created that tragedy. They must have wanted it. It must be for their own good, so I am not going to interfere. I am not going to judge them." This, the critics say, is irresponsible regardless of what the philosophy proposes.

Once again, the critics' observations and charges are correct about certain individuals who are part of the New Age. The naive, shallow, or expedient seekers will deny their own participation in human tragedy and adopt a non-involvement policy under the nobility of being non-judgmental.

We do not encourage being judgmental, either. However, many people are confused by the difference between being judgmental and having an opinion. Some people cannot distinguish between a preference and a judgment. In their zeal not to be judgmental, they have eliminated opinions and preference, too. It is not entirely their fault. They have been told not to be judgmental; they also have been taught, however, not to discern.

The honest seeker will accept responsibility for the reality creation and will also take steps to correct the inhumanity. The critic and the true seeker agree on this point: The inhumanity should be stopped.

The critic believes this because it's wrong and bad, the honest seeker believes this because those who suffer deserve the option of making other choices—they have the right to learn how to create happiness just like everyone else.

Consider for a moment. The critic says, "Outside forces are responsible for the tragic conditions in this world. I didn't create it, but I will work to fix it." The honest seeker of a new spirituality says, "Each person creates his own reality and is responsible for the tragic conditions in this world. I did create it, and I will work to fix it." Who is being more responsible?

RW: *Often the criticism is very direct. How do you tell a starving person that they created their own reality?*

We would not say that to a starving person. It is true, but we would never say that to a starving person until we did what was necessary to solve the problem. We would feed them first and then teach them how to create food for themselves, and then we would tell them about reality creation. Then and only then. It is inhuman to do otherwise.

You see, at one time your government thought the way to solve the ghetto problem was to pour money and more money into the rundown neighborhoods. Not soon enough, the officials began to realize that that approach did not work. In fact, it often made matters worse.

What did work? When the people who lived in the neighborhoods could participate in building their own homes, when they could take responsibility for and pride in their own reality, then progress was made. Yes, it took outside money to prime the pump. The pump was primed, and people started taking responsibility. They first learned that they could have a hand in creating their own reality.

Then they learned that they could create it all themselves. Some "bleeding heart" liberals—not all liberals, just one specific kind of liberal—did not like it very much when "those poor folks and blacks" took their power back. But they took their power back anyway!

What does the New Age person say to the starving person about creating their own reality? We would hope the honest seeker would have the sensitivity and insight to end the hunger, teach the starving person how to create ways to provide their own food, and then talk about reality creation.

RW: *Is the world going to come to an end sometime soon?*

No. We know there are many along the entire spectrum of spirituality who warn of the impending doom. The Fundamentalists point fervently to Revelations, often arguing over the fate of the Born Again. The interpretations vary depending upon whether you believe in pre-tribulation, mid-tribulation, or post-tribulation. At the other end of the spectrum, within the New Age there are those who spread the word of "doom and gloom."

From the mystic to the misfit, there are many who are sure the world is coming to an end. But, there have always been those who make such claims. Why is it more prevalent now?

1. Because you have what appears to be a "Rubik's Cube reality." Just when you find a solution to one problem, the very solution seems to create ten more problems. The only solution that makes sense to those with limited scope and limited vision is the non-solution: The end of the world.

Because "I cannot think of a solution, there must not be one." That thought gets institutionalized as philosophy.

Have you ever noticed what children do when they "play themselves into a corner"? They play in the sandbox, building "houses" and "roads" and play with their dolls and trucks. Then they run out of room, and they don't know what to do. Their solution: Just flatten the "roads" and smooth out all the "houses" and start over!

2. Life is more technologically advanced now, and it is also more complicated. Sometimes it is fun to get lost in a fantasy of starting over. How often have you heard people say just that, that they wish they could start over or that they long for the good old days when the world was simpler. For many it is much easier to romanticize about a world that ends, and then to wonder how they are going to be one of the few who will be smart enough or clever enough to survive. That fantasy is more "fun" than it is to worry about how to pay the mortgage, to question whether or not the kid really needs braces, or to find out if that white powder really was just Ajax—when did they start cleaning their bathroom?

The unreal world—even a world that ends—is sometimes more exciting than the real world of day-to-day.

3. Many of the economic forecasts, pollution pro-

jections, meteorological reports, and tectonics reports all predict doom. We agree there are problems. There are more problems than there are solutions right now. That does not mean the world is going to come to an end. It does mean that you have to find not only solutions, but you have to look for new ways of creating solutions to find. We did not say it would be simple, but that it is an intricate world does not mean it's a dead world.

4. All the ancient predictors of the future seem to end at or around the year 2000. The Egyptian pyramid and the Mayan calendar and the predictions of Nostradamus have two things in common: They have hitherto been very accurate, and all their predictions stop.

Many have taken that to mean that the world is about to end. To the contrary, we would suggest that the "stopped predictions" are just one more indication of the New Age.

You see, in the Old Age of Metaphysics you created your reality unconsciously and subconsciously. Therefore, predicting what you would create, though not easy by any measure, was possible for those who were sensitive. The ancient predictors were such sensitives.

In the New Age of Metaphysics and Spirituality you also create your own reality, except you do it consciously. Therefore, the true sensitive knows better than to try to predict what you will choose consciously.

An example: If you create a promotion at work in your subconscious, a psychic reader can tell you about a promotion they see for you and they might even be able to give you the dates. Though you have created this reality, you have done so in your subconscious mind. As yet, you know nothing about it consciously.

However, if you are going to consciously create that promotion, an honest psychic would not see it in your subconscious mind—because it is not there! Instead of telling you about a promotion you did not know about, he might tell you that you are thinking about creating a promotion for yourself. You can still have the thrill of being amazed!

The ancient oracles and seers could predict events that were imprinted on the subconscious minds of humankind. The sensitivity that allowed them to be so accurate was the same sensitivity that allowed them to know when to stop predicting. They knew a New Age was coming. They knew there was a time when predictions could not be made. They knew there would be a time when humankind would take back its own power.

They stopped predicting your future, because they knew it would be time for you to start creating it!

No, the world is not coming to an end. It is just beginning! Honestly, in ways you yet cannot understand, your world is just beginning!

You are alive at the most exciting time in all of history. You are standing at the brink, on the threshold of a whole new world. It's exciting. Have fun!

RW: *You seem to know so much about our world. Yet you state that you have never been physical. How can you know so much about our world? How can you know so much about us?*

Perhaps it would have been easier to say that we were once a person on your planet. We could have said that we lived in Atlantis, or maybe better yet, we could have claimed that we were from Lemuria. Maybe we could have just said that we were a monk from ancient Nepal. There would be no way to verify that

information. The problem: It's not true. We have this
thing about always telling the truth.

Also, in the carnival-like atmosphere that sur-
rounds much of the New Age, it would perhaps have
been easier to talk just like the channel and keep his
eyes open. Then the world would think that the channel was "a wonderfully bright fellow with a lot of
valuable insights." It would have been easier, but not
true.

We are not, nor have we ever been, physical. It may
be uncomfortable for people to understand or accept,
but it is true.

Well, how can we know so much about a world we
have never been "alive" in? In fact, our vantage point
often allows us to know more than if we had been
physical.

First, we can tap into the channel's memory banks
from this and any other lifetime. We can tap into your
memory banks, not to read your minds—no, we respect you too much for that—but to understand your
point of view. Jung spoke accurately of a collective
unconscious containing all the information from all
time about your world. We can tap into that if necessary.

Secondly, we exist outside of time. Therefore, the
multiple pasts and probable futures all exist for us in
what you call Now. Because we can see your past,
present, and future all at once, there can be a gestalt
of understanding and awareness that we can experience that you cannot. It does not make us better than
you, just more insightful.

Thirdly, and more importantly, we are not subject
to the physical plane of experiences, limitations, and
prejudices. Therefore, our information and insight can
more easily be uncluttered and free of the very mem-

ories and collective unconscious that we can tap into and not be unduly affected by.

Fourthly, mathematical set theory says that you cannot fully understand a set until you are outside of it. There are those who were once physical and are now outside the set of "all those who are currently physical." However, we are outside the set of "all those who have *ever* been physical," and therefore we are capable of a deeper level of insight about you and your world. However, evaluate us on the guidelines we have already discussed, not on our form—or, in this case, our lack of it!

Finally, some wonder how we can know your feelings if we have never been physical, how can we know your pain. Emotions are real. Your physical reality is an illusion, but the feelings you feel are real. Your emotions transcend all the illusion. Just because we have not generated the illusion in the form you have chosen does not mean we have not felt the feelings.

It is true that we never feel anger, hurt, fear, or even frustration, but we know those emotions. We do feel and know love. We can help you learn to feel love more strongly and completely than you know.

We can know you, and we can know your world because we love you, because we are committed to your growth, because we care.

RW: *I have one more question: Why are we here?*

That's a great question with which to conclude our discussion.

Many ask about the purpose, or mission, task. Others couch the question in terms of destiny. We use the word Focus.

We like the word because it more completely implies the choice that is involved. You see, no one gives you a task, mission, purpose. You choose it.

You decide what you want to "focus" on in each of your lifetimes. Like a lens of a camera, you can shift your focus at will. You can "zoom in" or you can find a "wide-angle shot." You can change the lens or use color filters. You can even focus on something else altogether.

There are two focuses, however, that always stay the same. These are the reasons people are people. These are the reasons you decided to manifest yourself in a physical form and why you chose to create yourself on the earth at this time.

First, to learn to have fun. That's right. To learn to have fun. And then, to learn to consciously create success. No, you are not here to suffer or struggle or to conquer pain. You are here to learn to have fun and to learn to consciously create success.

The emphasis is on the learning. It's not just being in the right place at the right time, knowing the right people, or being born into the right family. No, it's learning how to literally create a life that is fun; it is literally learning the steps and processes involved in consciously creating success.

Beyond learning, the focuses involve understanding fun and success. What "was fun" for you ten years ago is different from what you consider "is fun" now, which is still different from what you consider "will be fun" in twenty years from now. Like success, fun is ever-changing, ever-expanding.

Neither of these two focuses can be put on a "To Do" list. They are perpetual.

Beyond learning and understanding, there is balancing. You are here to also find the balance between long-term and short-term fun and success.

Finally, these focuses have to do with loving. All

the learning, understanding, and balancing in the world is not going to breathe life into the fun or the success you might create if the fun and success are not loving.

These two sound so simple, yet the number of life-times and the amount of pain in the world would suggest that not too many people really do know how to have fun or how to be consciously successful yet.

You see, you have this wonderful thing in your reality called Time. We know that most of you see time as the enemy. You blame it for three-quarters of the things you never have "time" for. You spend much of your life trying to reverse time to stay forever young. Though you often treat it like an enemy, time is actually a grand and valuable friend.

It is the cushion between the thoughts you think and the reality they create. Every thought that went through your head would be an instant reality if it were not for time, which gives you "time" to change your minds—or your thoughts.

Time is the net under the high-wire act of life. When you make a mistake, it catches you. You bounce rather than crash. Time gives you a second chance.

Without time, your life would be insane. Imagine for a moment that every thought you think happens *now!* As you are reading these words, an errant thought about sickness or death occurs, and you never even get to finish the sentence . . .

As you drive to work you have a stray thought about an auto accident and "you didn't even see them coming."

In a business meeting your mind wanders and in the midst of a daydream you vanish! Life would be insane!

While you are physical, you give yourself time and space and a past and a future to help you learn how to have fun and how to consciously create success.

Once you move to the higher levels—however you define them—there is no time. The bliss that is anticipated would truly be a hell.

You see, there are no judges who will decide whether you can evolve beyond the physical plane. There are no referees.

You are your own judge and referee. You will decide whether you are ready or whether you should return to learn a bit more about having fun. You will decide if you need to learn more about consciously creating your success.

Many want the reasons to be difficult or painful. Many want to see life as an ordeal that ennobles their struggle and their strife.

Please remember: Life is a gift. Life is a gift from God/Goddess/All That Is. Your real job is to learn how to receive.

It has been a pleasure talking with you. We close . . . with Love and Peace . . .

—Lazaris

J. Z. Knight/Ramtha

You need answers.
I am here to answer you.
　　　　　　　—Ramtha[1]

J. Z. Knight, the forty-year-old physical vehicle for the entity Ramtha, "the Enlightened One," is by far one of the most celebrated of all current channels. A housewife and former cable television executive, the tall, willowy blonde was first contacted by Ramtha in 1977 while experimenting with crystal pyramids on her kitchen table. J. Z. was reluctant to accept the entity at first. But after learning she was one of the warrior's ten children in a past life, and understanding that she could help a large number of people by acting as a channel, she finally agreed to cooperate. From the start of their project, Ramtha's words began spreading like wildfire, spearheading the current channeling movement.

Though J. Z.'s present life is one filled with acclaim and material rewards, her childhood was a grim story. Born in Roswell, New Mexico, J. Z. was still a young girl when her father, an alcoholic, deserted the family. Her mother raised the children alone. A strong belief in Fundamentalism kept the family together. As J. Z. has said, "I always loved God." She married early and had two sons, now nineteen and twenty-one. When that relationship turned sour, she divorced, and eventually married Jeffrey Knight, a dentist. Together they moved to Tacoma, Washington, where J. Z. had her first contact with Ramtha nine years ago.

Most New Age enthusiasts were first introduced to Ramtha in Shirley MacLaine's bestseller, *Dancing in the Light*. Ramtha, who is a 35,000-year-old warrior (a contemporary of Cro-Magnon man), helped answer not only MacLaine's spiritual questions but also offered suggestions that helped her to complete a dance performance after she had collapsed. He also advised MacLaine to alter her vitamin regimen.

Since his introduction to mainstream consciousness, Ramtha has attracted thousands of devotees, among them the actor Richard Chamberlain. In fact, Chamberlain was so moved by Ramtha's message, he agreed to host Knight's all-day sessions in his own Beverly Hills mansion during the early 1980s. But The Enlightened One is more than just a friend to the elite.

Ramtha is practically a household word thanks to the media's cooperation. He has spoken on *The Merv Griffin Show* and *Good Morning America* and has been heard by satellite in a dozen cities as diverse as Phoenix, Minneapolis and Kansas City. To reach an even wider audience, Knight travels twice a month to different areas of the country, spreading Ramtha's message. The entity usually appears in hotel ballrooms and draws as many as 400 participants eager to hear him speak. Ramtha Dialogues, staffed by fourteen dedicated workers, is the profit-making corporation that handles J. Z.'s publicity, seminars and the distribution of video tapes and cassettes. A book of Ramtha's philosophy is about to go into its third printing.

Frequently dressed in starched whites and surrounded by lavender flowers, J. Z. goes into a self-induced semiconscious state before she channels Ramtha, gyrates and then appears to go limp. "It's like a death process," Knight says about her channeling.

"I go through a tunnel, and there's a whistling sound and a light at the end." An instant before J. Z. leaves her physical body she raises the vibrational level of her soul to meet Ramtha's vibrations. Within moments, Knight "disappears" and Ramtha materializes. He strides back and forth, speaking in a low, clipped, rhythmic voice. Knight has described her trance by saying, "It's like taking a three-minute nap and waking up four hours later."

The channeler explains that the trance ends once she reaches the light. Knight claims she has virtually no memory of what the entity imparts and only learns later, by listening to taped recordings, of the wisdom imparted during her sessions.

After the channeling has been concluded, Knight finds it helpful to replenish herself by smoking a cigarette and drinking a Cherry Coke.

Ramtha, the Enlightened One, who claims to be (among other things) a warrior who conquered Atlantis, shares a message similar to many other entities who have been spreading the word. He stresses that God is not a remote entity but a part of everything in the universe, including humanity. Therefore, we are all divine beings and because of it, we are able to "create our own realities." Says Ramtha, "God the Father lives within us."

To further clarify the relationship, Ramtha has said, "God experiencing that which is termed Man, Man experiencing that which is termed God—am I a servant unto also. And who be divine enough to be that which is termed the tranquility of all things within His being? You!"

Ramtha also assures us that God is without judgment and therefore sees no evil: "God, the Father, the Magnificent, the Fabulous, the Miraculous, the Isness, the Totality, does not have an ego to judge good or bad. That was given to his beloved Son which all of you are, for only you possess the will of creativity. God, the Father, is the mass that you create from, but He hath created everything in a state of joy for He is all things."

He also points out, as do many spirit guides, that fear is the only force that limits our potential. "The great whore, as it were—Fear—enslaves and inhibits the creative mind. It does not permit love to bloom in its wondrous fields; it does not permit life to be reveled upon; it stagnates the emotion and kills hope."

Ramtha encourages boundless joy, self-reliance and inner strength. "Love what you are. Love the god that you are. Embrace the wind, and the willow, and the water, for it is the creation of your importance, and be at peace."

However, not all of Ramtha's messages are laced with optimism. In fact, the entity predicts a series of natural catastrophes in the form of earthquakes, hurricanes, tidal waves, volcanic eruptions, atmospheric pollution and polluted soil and water. For the next two decades, the entity warns, the earth will "cleanse and replenish" itself with these natural earthly disasters.

As a result of such doomsday predictions, many of Ramtha's followers have moved, with or without their families, to the Pacific Northwest, where Ramtha says it will be safe. He encourages them to live self-sufficiently, growing their own vegetable gardens, and stock-piling at least two year's worth of food while they wait for what he calls the "New Age of Super-consciousness in the year 2000." Real-estate agents estimate as many as 1,500 people have migrated to the area. The majority are single, middle-aged women.

In a 1986 article in *The New York Times*, Knight admitted her displeasure with the recent migration. "I don't want people moving to live near me," she said. "I love my small town the way it is. I'm not their leader. I'm not a guru; there are no such things as 'Ramtha-ites'; I'm not somebody's savior. This is a business."[2]

Statements such as these have caused doubters and the few dissatisfied clients to feel justified in their complaints about J. Z. Knight's integrity. Indeed, the channeler's lifestyle in her brick mansion on the Yelm, Washington, multimillion-dollar ranch have led some skeptics, and former adherents, to raise their eye-brows.

In their spare time, Knight and her husband care for sixty valuable Arabian horses and drive their pow-der-blue Rolls-Royce through the countryside. These opulent items are paid for in full by Ramtha readings, seminars and other paraphernalia.

A weekend workshop usually costs $400 and a week-long desert retreat runs $1,200. So popular are the sessions that on an average, Ramtha Dialogues grosses between $100,000 and $200,000 for an evening's work.

The channel is hardly fazed by her critics, and ad-mits readily that she earns millions of dollars a year from personal appearances and the sale of "Ramtha-mobilia." J. Z. not only points out that 50 percent of her profits are taxable (since she is not a registered religious organization), but also explains that "It takes a lot of money to do what we do. It's an exchange of energy for energy."

Elwood Babbitt

Each of you upon his journey should see that which exists beyond his limitations. He should express freedom of spirit and arise to proclaim in a convincing manner where his spirit now is, telling in all honesty of a stronger awareness, admitting no error along the way so that you in your spirit and you in the flow of creativity can meld as one with the creative forces of all energy.

—Socrates (through Elwood Babbitt)

Probably no channel is more closely attuned with the works of the great medium Edgar Cayce than Elwood Babbitt. The diversity and accomplishments of this channeler are impressive. Although Babbitt does not keep records, it is estimated by Charles H. Hapgood, Elwood's biographer, that between 100 and 150 individual personalities have emerged in Babbitt's trance state. Among the prominent entities who have voiced their messages through this channel are: Christ, Vishnu, Albert Einstein, Socrates, Winston Churchill, Sigmund Freud, Krishna, Abraham Lincoln, Michael the Archangel and William Wordsworth.

Like Cayce, Babbitt had a minimal formal education. Born in Orange, Massachusetts, on November 22, 1922, Elwood was a bored and distracted student. As a result, he never finished high school. Occupied throughout his childhood with the spirit world, he often played with spirit children rather than with his peers. While serving in the military, his psychic gifts were often manifested, especially while he was under extreme emotional or physical pressure. He recalled one such experience during his combat days at Guadalcanal and Saipan.

"I'd seen men beside me that were fatally wounded and yet the spirit was so strong and the physical so intent that the spiritual part would pick up—actually pick up—the physical weapon and keep moving ahead. Once I made the mistake of saying to one fellow at my side, 'What're you doing here when your body is back there?' And we both turned and looked, and he looked at me in disbelief, and then he just faded and the rifle dropped to the ground."[4]

Elwood Babbitt is a trance medium and while giving readings sits in a straight-backed chair, closes his eyes and goes into a sleep-like state. He reports that his own spirit leaves his body and another one then takes possession. Babbitt reports that not all entities come from the same level. "In the outer circles," he says, "there is only positive energy; but in the nearer circles negative energies exist. Therefore, it is necessary to make a clear channel from the outer progression through to the earth level."

The entity takes a while to adjust itself to the new form, but once it does, Babbitt's voice and facial expressions change. At the end of the trance, Babbitt has absolutely no recall of what has transpired.

During his contact with other spirit entities, Babbitt is aided by controls: Jim Cole, who helps with physical and practical problems, and Dr. Frederick Fisher, an especially educated control who often shares answers to philosophical dilemmas. Fisher's sophisticated use of language is markedly different from Babbitt's own informal speech. Either Fisher or Cole appear to be responsible for helping to facilitate the entrance of the visiting entities. Frequently, the controls come through themselves and act as commentators during the readings. Krishna also makes occasional visits, and holds the highest vibrational level of the three.

While conscious and not in a trance, Babbitt reads auras and can give Life Readings of past lives (all held in complete confidentiality). He occasionally predicts the future as well. Also a gifted psychometrist, he can, while holding a physical object in his hands, locate and pick up thoughts of the person who previously handled it.

Babbitt lives with his wife, Emily (gifted clairvoyantly as well), and their children on his farm in Northfield, Massachussetts. He likes to refer to himself as a farmer, and certainly dresses the part, but only a small portion of his land is cultivated. He is too occupied during the day with the readings to take on the responsibility of cultivating a larger piece of land.

In his daily life, at every moment, Babbitt reads auras. In fact, most of the time, he does not see the physical bodies of people who are standing in front of him. He understands them by the aura patterns—lights and colors—that surround their physical beings. Babbitt explained the nuances of aura-reading to Hapgood in these terms:

"The main life color is deep blue. And it's about two inches wide. If you become exceedingly angry the red in your aura will expand to a six- to eight-inch width. If it gets up to a width of, say, ten inches this leads to temporary insanity. As your anger recedes, the vibration evens off."[5]

Babbitt is not interested in using his mediumship to become wealthy or famous. He channels from a desire to reach a religious attunement with God. He attributes his focus to his father, who often told him, "Always seek the highest, and you will never have serious troubles in your life."

Pat Rodegast/Emmanuel

Be comforted
and walk your life in Light and trust
for nothing will come to you
that is not meant to be.
There is nothing that can happen in your
life
that in any way threatens your soul.
Indeed, all of life experience
enhances its awareness.
There is nothing that does not serve
the process of the soul's growth.

—Emmanuel[6]

Fourteen years ago, Pat Rodegast was sitting in Transcendental Meditation when out of the corner of her inner vision she witnessed a being of golden light. After a week's time, the vision moved directly in front of her, consuming her entire consciousness. "Who are you?" she asked. The being said simply, "I am Emmanuel." From that moment, the journey of enlightenment began for Pat Rodegast.

"When I first saw an inner vision, I knew it wasn't my imagination, and I had to make a choice—either that's reality or it's not," Pat explains. "And if that wasn't a reality, then I was in trouble. So I chose to believe it, and once I did that, I had to honor it."

Pat Rodegast is a channeler who lacks any spiritual pretentiousness. She is earthy, easily amused, good-natured, open and joyful. When channeling, she does not have a peculiar voice, a different accent, strange gestures, nor does she display any manners strikingly varied from her own. Ram Dass wrote in his intro-duction to *Emmanuel's Book:* "From my point of view as a psychologist, I allow for the theoretical possibil-ity that Emmanuel is a deeper part of Pat . . . In the final analysis, what difference does it really make?"

Pat explains that Emmanuel says his reality is al-ways with her and that it "bounces up and down. When I go into that state, when I meditate, there's a oneness. When I channel Emmanuel I also get a view-point that I would never have thought of. At the same time, it also sounds familiar. I don't know if it feels familiar because it is truth and I'm spinning into it— or because somewhere I'm connecting on another level."

When she channels, Pat hears Emmanuel's words and then forgets them. "It doesn't go through a thought process. It's spontanenous. It seems as though the part of me that is human personality, that steps aside, is the same part of me that has to record and put things into a structure of who I am supposed to be in this lifetime. So when that's disconnected, five minutes pass, and I just don't remember what Emmanuel has said."

In fact, so many of Emmanuel's words fade from Rodegast's consciousness that when she was compil-ing transcriptions along with Judith Stanton for *Em-manuel's Book*, she remembers being "very excited about what I was seeing for the first time." The book, originally planned as a vanity publication ("Christmas presents for friends"), sold 50,000 copies almost instantly—much to Rodegast and Stanton's surprise and delight. The book is now being printed and distributed by a major publishing house.

Emmanuel's message is upbeat, positive, filled with inexhaustible joy and liberating hope. When it comes to the possibility of nuclear destruction he says we have a choice—to choose love or fear. No matter how reasonable fear is, it's an illusion. He tells us that this is a place to choose love where love seems not to be.

Pat says, "Emmanuel doesn't buy into *Oh wow*. He just doesn't bite. When someone says to him, 'Give me a miracle, give me an Oh wow,' Emmanuel says, 'Your whole life is a miracle. Your whole life is an Oh wow. The planet is a schoolroom and school isn't over until the last soul graduates.' He doesn't feed fear—and he's right.

"Fear," Pat cautions, "has learned to talk the language of love, so don't be fooled by it. The whole nuclear disarmament movement is being fueled from a place of fear, not love."

During Pat and Emmanuel's workshops (she no longer channels private sessions) the thread of love is predominant, but neither the channel nor her guide allows for any dependence by the members of the audience. "Emmanuel keeps handing it back," Pat says. "He never tells anyone what to do. If he does make predictions, it's always very generalized. He will explore reasons about why you may be afraid to decide for yourself. He's a teacher. He says, 'I wouldn't tell you if I knew—because you're not a puppet—you're God.' He won't let anybody lean."

Currently, Emmanuel is focusing a great deal of energy on AIDS patients—and has suggested to Pat that she publish the transcripts of these workshops. Emmanuel says that AIDS is also fear. "We manufacture diseases because we need a place to put our fear. We need to know the nature of things and to overcome them with love."

Emmanuel tells us, "Hearts are yearning to hear truth now, for the world has so frightened itself by the nuclear threat, by the illnesses that seem to sweep across the land that fear has come to the edge of its own destruction. And the hearts are saying, 'No, no, this cannot be all there is.' The moment you are willing to hear, the universe will speak to you."

Rodegast doesn't doubt for a moment that we are all capable of coming into contact with our own "Emmanuel." She insists every one of us can follow our spiritual journey—one needn't be wealthy to do so. Pat is a bit disheartened by the current cost of channeling. "I try not to judge when other channelers charge a lot of money, because everyone has their own path. On the other hand, I feel uncomfortable charging a lot. I don't think it should be just for the rich." In keeping with her philosophy, many of Pat's workshops cost $10, intensive weekends with room and board under $200, and the cost of her video and audio tapes are well within reason.

Pat explains that some people think those channels who are in it just for the money will lose their guide. "Nonsense! I don't think if I do anything wrong there will be a thunderbolt. Emmanuel says karma is not a balancing of books. We're here to remember who we are and to become our Oneness. People get outraged when he says that. During a workshop someone once said 'You mean I have to be one with the soul of Hitler!' Emmanuel answered, 'My dear, when you and Hitler are ready to become one, all of the animosity will have been altered to Light and Truth.'

If you were to climb the highest mountain
and look at your world,
you would see
much more Light than darkness
much more love than hate,
much more kindness than violence.
It is only that these negative areas
are more vocal.
They are calling for help.
They are like small children, lost and fearful.
Knowing not what else to do,
they shout and scream and strike out.

Pray for them.
Pray for all of them
and do not fear."[7]

Alexander Murray

The human salmon is like Hamlet, "To Be or Not To Be." It doesn't know whether to be a human or a salmon. All that thinking will really make you crazy, won't it?

—Bright Star

"I'm a rare medium," Alexander Murray says with characteristic humor. Despite the fact that at forty-three he is probably one of the busiest, most recognized and documented channelers in the United States, Murray maintains an accessible and down-to-earth demeanor. He is a popular channeler who actually answers his own telephone.

During the fifteen years of his career, during which time he conducted approximately 3,000 sessions, Alex has been the subject of numerous research projects and is one of television's most frequently taped telepaths. For the American Society for Psychical Research, he successfully demonstrated clairvoyance, psychokinesis and astral projection while a CBS–TV crew filmed the out-of-body experiments. As a guest of the Parapsychology Society, he gave thirty trance

demonstrations at the United Nations. He was taped
in trance for ABC's *Morning Show* and for the same
network's *Eyewitness News*. The media were so impressed with his abilities that NBC hired Murray as
a consultant for their soap, *Search for Tomorrow*. Their
ratings jumped.

Murray travels frequently. Our appointment was
sandwiched between his return from London and his
trip to Peru. Murray makes his home on New York
City's Upper West Side. His apartment is furnished
with expensive elegance: plush carpeting, Japanese
prints and brocade kimonos on the walls; Buddhas
poised on tables; a fresh bouquet of white gladioli in
a brass vase. Murray is fastidious about his surround-
ings (no pens allowed while sitting on the couch—
only pencils); visitors must leave their shoes in the
hall.

His apartment is filled three evenings a week with
approximately fifteen students who buy their seats on
a monthly subscription basis. In between, he gives
private readings. Murray begins each session, about
two hours in length, with a group prayer meditation
and, as he puts it, "Some OMs, mostly to get the students in the right place. I go into a trance
like . . . [Murray snaps his fingers]." After only seconds of silence, Murray slumps forward, swallows a
gasp of air, then sits back in his chair and returns as
the embodiment of a spirit guide. "The predictable is
not what happens," says the channeler. "It's very
spontaneous because there's no agenda for the spirits."

The session I attended manifested a cast of approximately a half dozen different guides as well as
Murray's "Master of Ceremonies"—Bright Star—a
laughing, slightly offbeat spirit with an effeminate
voice and a sometimes silly way of making his point.

Most of the students seemed to recognize their personal guides, who sported several different accents and mannerisms: American Indian, Oriental, Hindu, ancient Greek, etc. The group welcomed their appearance in unison, but each student asked personal questions of his or her personal guide. Once their questions—ranging from a concern for aging (the woman was thirty-one) to the specific path for spiritual fulfillment—were satisfactorily answered, the spirit said his farewell. Murray then slumped forward again, and after seconds passed, another entity would rise.

Murray's spiritual entities (none of whom he remembers, since he is in a total trance state) discuss, among other subjects, the importance of recognizing the God within ourselves; the perils and pitfalls of fear; and living within the moment—not thinking about it. Bright Star says, "When you get into 'What does it mean?' you detach from 'How does it feel?' And how it feels is really what it means. If you can't feel, forget it."

When the spirit White Hawk speaks, he tells a woman who appears to have just ended a relationship, "We have to make you strong and confident because we have good work to do. Once we learn to take care of ourselves, we can go out and have fun." The woman nods in agreement and smiles. White Hawk appears to have answered a question no one else in the room hears.

After two hours, and a long series of messages from various guides, Alex slumps forward for the final time and the group ends the session with a melodic chant. Immediately thereafter, the students stand silently and leave. No one just "hangs around," waiting to speak to Murray.

"I'm not into greed or power, and I don't want to

run anyone's life," explains Murray. "I was never a follower and I don't want anyone following me. I never liked the guru trip. I don't want a cast of thousands around me.

"I like gourmet meals," Alex says as an analogy. "Twenty-five or thirty nice people with taste, to meet in quiet, elegant circumstances is all I'm looking for. I'm an elitist, not a snob. I just like to work with people on a certain level."

Murray prefers to teach and run workshops. "When I'm channeling, my creative needs as Alex aren't being fulfilled, because I'm unconscious, I'm asleep. Teaching helps me to be connected to my work." And, says Murray putting modesty aside, "I'm probably one of the few channels who can *really* teach."

Pete A. Sanders, Jr.

When someone else is doing your channeling, it just puts one more interference
before you. Like the game "Telephone,"
the message gets distorted along the
way.

Pete A. Sanders, Jr., is a man with a mission: Debunk
the myth that only the spiritually select can channel.
Claims Sanders, "*Anyone* can do it." How? Study the
scientifically-based curriculum, practice with the right
attitude and attend his workshops (at only $10 a ses-
sion). The thirty-six-year-old president and founder of
Free Soul, a tax-exempt educational facility in Sedona, Arizona, has already taught over 25,000 people
to self-channel.

Growing up in Southern California, Pete naturally
developed an interest in ESP and other paranormal
phenomena. But there was a snag: Even though he
was astounded and impressed by the psychically as-
tute he found that he himself had very little natural
ability. "One of the biggest myths in the field is that
only a few people are gifted, and I fell for it."

But in 1975, Sanders had his first breakthrough. He

took a class on aura vision in the LA area and discovered that with the proper training he was indeed
able to see auras. To date, this is still his strongest
psychic ability. "I found that yes, I was one of the less
naturally gifted psychically, but I was able to train
myself to overcome my handicap. Now I'm a complete
believer that anyone can learn," Sanders says.

"Everyone has some aspect they can develop. But
people tend to feel that if they're not naturally gifted
they have to go to someone else. That's just not so.
They can learn."

A scientist by nature, Sanders attended MIT, ma-
joring in biomedical chemistry with a minor in brain
science. He began to concentrate on biofeedback experiments. Although mainstream today, at the time
biofeedback was considered far-out. Sanders discovered that if people focused on one particular area of
their body, they could effect a dramatic change. It
was especially helpful in teaching migraine sufferers
to dilate their own blood vessels and thereby relieve
their painful symptoms.

"Then it dawned on me," Pete recalls. "I thought,
there must be places in the body that you can focus
on to increase psychic activity. That was the second
breakthrough. While I was working on my own at
MIT, I discovered what I call the body's psychic reception areas."

According to Sanders, the psychic reception areas
are the focal points for the psychic antennae of the
body. One of them is the third eye; another is in the
solar plexus; the other two, for intuition and direct
voice hearing, are more complicated to locate. "Once
people realize where these centers are," says Sanders,
"They can learn to pick up a psychic signal even if
it's on low volume. Psychically gifted people hear
messages at full blast. But for the less gifted, it's a

way for them to tune in and pick up communications that might be more difficult to hear. For the first time, they can learn to experience psychic signals."

Sanders was so excited by his discovery, he turned down his acceptance to Harvard Medical School and began to develop his theories. As part of his research, he traveled around visiting psychics. Two things distressed him. He was naturally disappointed by the con artists and frauds, but he was also disturbed by the sincere channelers. "I was upset by the dependency it created. Clients were being trained to think they had to go to that source, not trained to develop their own abilities."

In order to put his discoveries into action, and to help dispel the myth that only some possess the key to channeling, Pete Sanders founded Free Soul. The public education and public service center, with 200 teachers nationwide, claims to have taught 90 percent of its clients to self-channel successfully. Its foundation is scientific, not mystical. "People can believe what they want to," says Pete. "If they prefer to describe it spiritually or mystically, that's okay. But I come from a perspective of practical skepticism. In other words, the best way to do anything is to prove it to yourself. Then you know for sure.

"Science says that every thought, every brain wave, every wave of light that ever shone in the universe is still shining somewhere. That's scientific *fact* and it means that it's possible to tap into any force. In fact, when Einstein was asked later in his life where he got his ideas, he said, 'I've learned to tap into the universal consciousness.' That's what this is all about."

Sanders agrees that the latest developments are reflective of an evolution of consciousness, but he is quick to point out that consciousness has always evolved. "Only today, it's accelerating." The scientific channel points to the new physics as a foundation for his own practice. "Superstarian physicists, for example, claim that everything exists in ten dimensions, simultaneously. Therefore," says Pete, "it's another way out for people to open the windows onto higher dimensions. The windows are always there."

Sanders says that self-channeling is the field of Inner Human Technology. "Today, there are three great scientific frontiers: Space, Ocean and—Inner Human Technology. When it comes to IHT, everyone can be a pioneer. Everyone can be his or her own explorer."

Judith Hope Davis

I am not only one with this Spirit, but
this Spirit is all that I am. It is my whole
being, and this Divine Wisdom is in my
thought, causing me to act and move
intelligently, to make right choices and
to follow right pursuits. There are no
problems in this Divine Wisdom.

Advice to those who seek out Judith Hope Davis: ex-
pect nothing out of the ordinary—prepare for the most
extraordinary. If this seems a contradiction, it's appropriate. Judith is by far one of the most remarkable
and versatile channels practicing in this country, yet
her presentation and communication is down-to-earth,
warm, unpretentious. If you allow yourself to open
for her psychic adventure, you're in for quite a joy-
filled and educational ride.

  With nothing more than a brief handshake and hello,
Judith, a slight woman in her thirties, reaches over
and turns on a cassette machine to tape the session.
She sits in an upholstered rocking chair and begins
to move back and forth, her head swaying from side
to side. Her voice remains her own (no entity takes

over her body), though she speaks in an airy, monot-
onous rhythm. She explains that during the reading
the aura is opened and there is an increase in prana—
the basic vital energy upon which life on earth is con-
structed. After the reading, the aura is closed but the
prana is heightened and remains so for approximately
three days.

"In my opinion," says Davis, "that's the best part
of being here. This energy will be available for you to
touch and use over the next few days. You can use it
to facilitate expansion of thought, facilitate healing
physically, emotionally, mentally for yourself, your
loved ones; to facilitate increase in understanding,
peace in your relationship, international concerns,
world peace. Enjoy that."

She welcomes questions, allows notetaking and will
permit the reading to follow under the direction of
her client. Davis explains that she is conscious, though
in an altered state of consciousness, during the readings. She once described the sensation she experiences
as "flipping fast-forward through a book filled with
visual pages of past, present and future lives."

Davis can not only read a client's past life, but can
on suggestion locate a friend, lover or relative of the
client with only the name, city and state of residence.
She will then read their present physical and emotional condition, as well as their past lives. During
my session, her readings of friends located quite a
distance away were remarkably accurate.

Those who have known Judith for several years claim
that she lives separately from the material world, existing most of her waking and sleeping hours on the
astral plane. When she looks at another human being
she reads their aura instantly. As a result of her highly
sensitive gifts, Judith leads a hermetic life. She rarely

leaves her home—doesn't see movies, go to the supermarket or travel.

The channel and her husband, Jim Davis (a psychic healer who specializes in etheric cleansings), are the founders of the Life and Light Centre, a facility situated deep in the northern Vermont woods. Thirteen people live on the 300-acre farm, although most hold jobs outside the Centre. The main house, where readings and healings take place, is a simple wooden structure decorated with large crystals, amethysts and plants.

Nina Lynn, Ph.D. and Director of Special Education for Newfane, Vermont, has been seeing Judith for several years and feels strongly that Judith is tuned in directly to "the Source." "Judith always gives me what I need to work on, not just those pretty little generic sayings. Her predictions are almost always accurate, although the individual must do the work to make them happen. If you take the words and work on them, you become cleaner, happier, joy-filled—more embracing of life."

"A person's choices very often reflect past conditions, different societies, different conditions," Judith explains, "as one makes choices based upon previous life expression. For example, an individual who spent several incarnations in Nepal or the Himalayan area might be more inclined towards the use of mind-altering drugs. This was used in that society to achieve illumination. So in this way, an entity makes choices."

Although many people have been seeing Judith for guidance for a dozen years, she discourages dependency and does not have contact with her clients outside the sessions, which last for an hour and must be booked in advance of a year (sometimes longer). One would be advised to ask her assistant, Robbie, to put you on the waiting list for possible cancellations.

"Understand that we are now in a phase of transition into New Age consciousness; we are not yet *in* New Age consciousness," explains Davis. "This transition was very much brought about, the trigger, during the period of Pope Nicholas I, wherein the holy mysteries of Christianity were revoked. This plunged the Western world into materialism. Now we have a transition from materialism to a more spiritual reality. So what we find, quite naturally, is spiritual materialism. We are moving towards a dharmic state of consciousness, but we have not yet achieved this."

When asked how one can differentiate between "real channels" and the "less gifted," Davis replies: "It has become, on this planet, a fad situation. There are few, shall we use the term 'real,' and there are many who are merely signposts. They do point a way. And there is value in everything. All things work together for good. Nothing is bad. It's only how we perceive it that makes it so.

"This is, of course, associated with an immortal perspective, as opposed to the mortal, one-time frame. It is a dilemma. One can only suggest you listen to your own heart. This is really your only guide. The truth you find within your heart."

Susan Chicovsky/Enoch

There has been much blame, suffering, pain and wars upon the earth. The Aquarian Age is the age of enlightenment, harmony, peace and growth. We do not recognize a World War III as such. What we sense is that there will be a clearing upon the earth. How this will manifest is not clear at this time. The choice has not been made by humans— though there are many humans working with themselves, working to understand that they are God, and God is within them, that they are a soul with a body.

—Enoch

Susan Chicovsky, a petite, round-faced woman in her thirties, is leading a group through meditation and prayer. She gently asks those assembled to visualize walking up a long line of stairs. At the top, she tells them, they will find a door. "But," Susan points out with the loving patience of a mother to her children, "notice that it's not quite time to move through the door yet. We have thirteen years left before the New Age officially arrives and manifests. What's happening now is that the time is available to stand in the doorway and experience the truth of the past and the future simultaneously in the present."

It is obvious to those who visit or listen to Chicovsky, either on tape or during one of her many radio appearances, that one of her primary focuses is the coming of a new millennium. She has no problem identifying herself with the New Age. "We're ending a 2,000-year period of consciousness called the Piscean Age and specifically, right now, we're ending a 5,000-year cycle. So we're opening up our hearts in a new way.

"For the next thirteen years [until 2000], you have a choice to remain within yourself and to let go of all the distractions around you. The distractions may come—we're not saying there won't be mind-talk, pain, murders—but their importance lies in how much power you give them. It's how much attention or focus you choose to put on the outside—and how much you choose to put on the inside."

In preparation for the coming of the Aquarian Age, Susan facilitates "inside" work and the opening of hearts by employing techniques such as channeling, crystal use, dowsing with a pendulum, meditation, hands-on healing, sealing, grounding and breath work. "Words," she explains, "aren't enough."

Susan was first introduced to her spirit guide, Enoch, while under a hypnotic state induced by a psychologist who was trying to discover the cause of her back pain. For a few years following, Susan would act as the physical vehicle for Enoch but was uncertain and physically uncomfortable when she totally lost consciousness and her body and voice transformed. More distressing was the fact that Enoch would sometimes manifest spontaneously.

Finally Susan requested that the knowledge come *through* her, while she was conscious, only when she asked for it and only when it would be beneficial to others. Now Susan is in communication with a series of guides (Abraham, Kaki, etc.) who call themselves "overseers." They channel energy through Enoch, who then moves through Susan.

She does not pay too much attention to guide identification because she feels that it is the "energy that is important, not the dramatics. There is such a blending of energy between my guides and myself that there's very little distinction. We're together all the time. I live in that space. It's a constant lifestyle.

"The information Enoch shares is pure in my heart. It doesn't deal with the devil, there's no ritual, no satan, no cult. We help empower people. We ask them to get in touch with their higher selves."

Chicovsky asks her clients to come prepared for their private sessions with a series of six to eight questions. The waiting time for an appointment is between four and six months. Many of her clients, both nationally and internationally, who can't make it to Susan's home in Evergreen, Colorado, conduct their sessions over the telephone. Susan then mails them a tape of the reading.

Along with her husband, Tom, Susan also holds weekly group meetings under the banner of their organization, Vision Light. The evening classes include live channeled music by "The Light Brigade" (a New Age band), meditation and a sharing of information and resources. The focus is on self-awareness and includes a question-and-answer period at the end of the class.

Three months a year, Susan and her husband travel across the country giving classes on topics ranging from "experiencing personal life force" to "the role of religion," while granting interviews to the media and holding private channeling sessions.

"Channeling is an experience and an expression of truth and life simultaneously. There's no separation," Susan says. "That's why it isn't a big deal, and it's not just something only a few can do. My guides told me that what I do is a birthright. It's not a psychic or spiritual gift. All we can do is to help facilitate people back to their birthright.

"We've separated ourselves from our hearts and our instincts. People stopped trusting and believing in themselves and God. The real message is to let yourself shine. The shining comes from inside and out. Now it's time to return to the Source. The Reunion is happening now."

Mark Victor Venaglia/ Benjamin

My friends, never run! Seek out the problem and solve it. Melt the polar ice caps of the hearts of the victims of AIDS. Look unto that word: AIDS. AIDS. It is tangible evidence. This can be solved by sunrise. Say unto each person: *Love Yourself!* Merely. This is all. This is the matter at hand for each disease, but mostly this one.

—Benjamin

The monthly group sessions that Mark Victor Venaglia channels in his New York City loft draw about three hundred people. A suggested $10 donation covers the price of admission and a plate of organic food. The channel also suggests you bring your own blanket and pillow. (Though the loft is 1,700 square feet, it's still a tight squeeze.) The sessions begin at one in the afternoon, but people are encouraged to stay as long as they feel the need. Some do, mingling well into the early morning hours. If this sounds like a psychic's Woodstock, you're right: Mark Venaglia very much reflects the notion chanted two-decades ago, that "All You Need Is Love." But Venaglia's message has a mediumistic twist that tunes into the spirit entity of Benjamin Franklin—"Ben," as Mark calls him affectionately.

This channel, like J. Z. Knight, who is passionate about the Pacific Northwest, feels a special connection to the island of Manhattan. He is certain that New York is laying the groundwork for the spiritual movement. "The rest of the country," he says, "will take its tone from Manhattan." If one wonders how Venaglia could overlook the intense channeling activity in California, he has the answer and it dates back to Atlantis.

"In Atlantis, the law of karma was simple," he explains. "Where something begins, it ends. It's all the same. Atlantis ended with the majority of the population using its psychic abilities for self-motivating factors *only*, without any regard for the balance of the earth. You just can't take and take from the earth, whether it's minerals or energy, without there being an imbalance. The imbalance occurred and that set off the fault lines beneath the continent. Atlantis sank."

Venaglia contends that right now, in New York, everyone who was alive in Atlantis during those days 2,000 years ago, has either moved to, or been incarnated, in Manhattan and its surrounding areas. "That's why," he says, "we have thousands of New Yorkers tuning into channeling."

Ben, the spirit guide, has a voice that emanates from a rectangle that exists alongside Venaglia's right shoulder, up his neck. As if listening to an electronic speaker, Mark is able to hear Ben's words, repeating them almost simultaneously to his rapt clientele, many of whom are gay and afflicted with AIDS. Ben makes it perfectly clear that he understands the cause of the illness (the spirit prefers to use the term *bereavement*), understands how to help people heal themselves, and also "knows" and can identify (although not by her legal name) the woman doctor who will find the cure.

An AIDS transcript, channeled through Venaglia by Ben, has helped to cure several AIDS patients. George Melton and Will Garcia, both no longer showing AIDS symptoms, are avid Ben enthusiasts and are scheduled to appear on ABC's *20/20* to tell of their recovery through the help of Benjamin Franklin.

The following are excerpts from the transcript of what Venaglia terms Ben's AIDS "manifesto," taped on July 16, 1985:

"It is an ancient disease made noble through man's pathetic inability to care about his brethren. That is why it manifests itself these days. You with more aptitude, I bring you the skills to sharpen your own abilities in order to remove from excess the negative feelings which create the thoughts, which in turn create this bereavement.

"Those who seek out this bereavement called AIDS, and indeed know they seek it out for themselves, are bringing upon themselves the opportunity to chastise all those in their immediate physical circle. Those with AIDS must come to be thought of as healers. Look at the good. Look at the fortuitous circumstances that have first been brought forward because of this circumstance. Brother embracing brother, yes!

"Those that manifest AIDS are a blessed race, descended from the island of Crete and Gettys, a smaller island off the coast, southwest of the Atlantean continent; an entire civilization of healers and nobles.

"Ask them if they have dreams in which they are wrapped in translucent white sheets. This is a dream common to all AIDS victims, desperately trying to remind themselves of a civilization they were once a part of."

Ben not only points out relationships to the past, but points a menacing finger at today's conservative medical profession: "AIDS seeks to polarize beliefs within the medical profession. Unto these so-called patriots of healing, I say to them: *Beware!* For *all* that they have created seeks them now! Ruthlessly . . . Caution your own friends within the medical profession, for the days of holistic healing are upon us."

The savior who will find the cure for AIDS is the woman doctor Ben refers to in sessions as "Beth." She will, he says, meld together the metaphysical and medical aspects. Ben describes her as "lovely, slightly overweight, a full-bosomed babe." He suggests we "send her the strength that she is able to find her own wisdom."

As far as Venaglia the channel is concerned, AIDS is the cornerstone of the spiritual movement. Because of AIDS and those who heal themselves, he feels, the entire human race will come to realize that the power is within. "Doctors can only facilitate," he says. "AIDS is as challenging and as easy to heal as the common cold. The orthodox medical profession will not produce the cure for AIDS because the cure already exists. We can heal ourselves."

Venaglia and his following—or, as Ben calls them, "revolutionaries within the spiritual revolution"—are busy creating a healing center called Miracle on West 24th Street, in the channel's converted factory building. The five-story building will house the elderly and AIDS victims, an Artists' Collective, the Healing Theatre, a yoga center specializing in classes for pregnant women, a healing resource center that will refer clients to massage therapists, Past Life psychotherapists, Bach Flower Remedy practitioners and other New Age professionals, as well as an organic food café on the ground floor. The idea for Miracle on West 24th Street and its small publishing company, Olde Benjamin's Press, which publishes Mark's channeling transcripts, was proposed by Benjamin Franklin. "Ben stresses *doing*," says Venaglia. "We're incarnated in a physical body so that we can do . . . take action, make things happen."

But seeing what will happen in the future is not one of the aspects of channeling that Mark or Ben feel is important. "The whole idea of psychic work and channeling is *not* to produce predictions, choose winning Lotto numbers or Wall Street stocks. That does not help people change their value system. And the reason the planet is in trouble is because people do not value love," Venaglia says.

"The real bolt of the spiritual movement is educating the planet into self-love and belief in the impossible. Ben tells us to believe in our dreams—and make them real."

Sanaya Roman/Orin

Enlightenment is about remaining constantly open. As you gain this constancy, information flows from the higher realms clearly into your right-brain receptive mind, and is interpreted accurately by your left-brain analytical mind. You are aware of each moment and that awareness is the doorway into higher consciousness. Enlightenment is within your reach. You already have it . . .

—Orin[8]

When Sanaya (pronounced Sah-nay-ah) Roman was eighteen years old, she was told by a psychic that she would be a channeler. Although the idea sounded intriguing, Sanaya was soon caught up in the material world. Upon graduating Phi Beta Kappa from the University of California at Berkeley, she focused on the practical and began her own marketing consultation business. "I loved the business world," she says, "but it seemed as if something were missing." Around the same time, Jane Roberts was channeling Seth. To fill in the missing piece in her life, Sanaya gathered some friends together to study the Seth books and to experiment with the Ouija board.

In 1977, while Sanaya was employing the Ouija, Orin introduced himself. He explained that Sanaya would be communicating with him for many years to follow, but first she had to grow. Although she continued to hear from Orin, Dan, another guide on a lower vibrational level, came through more frequently.

Not long after the start of her Ouija board experiences, Sanaya was in a serious automobile accident. Her car was overturned. She flew out of the car, miraculously landing right side up. "As my car was turning over on the freeway, time was greatly slowed and doorways seemed to open onto other dimensions." Because of that breakthrough, Sanaya felt confident enough to put the Ouija board aside and began to channel through her voice.

But in the beginning Orin still hesitated to come through directly. He explained, through Dan, that Sanaya's body was like an electrical wire that could only handle twenty volts. Orin's voltage reached around fifty. "The first time I tried to let Orin come through, I almost passed out," Sanaya explains. "I felt like I was expanding from top to bottom, becoming sponge-like, larger than the room, but still encased in an energy field."[9]

In order to develop her capacity, Orin told her to practice speaking the same speed as a heartbeat by using a metronome to gain the correct tempo, to pay attention to her breath and to increase her concentration through specific exercises. Sanaya was an enthusiastic and dedicated student and within three years Dan left, and she was able to channel directly with Orin.

"I experience Orin as a very loving, wise, gentle being with a distinct presence," Sanaya has written. "While I am conscious, I am not able to affect the words as they come through me. I can stop them, but I can't add my own words or change the message."

Orin's message strongly suggests that we should all follow our inner voice and contact our higher selves. He stresses that ultimately, we are totally responsible for our lives. "You are a wise and wonderful being, and I see in all of you the desire to grow, to love, live with joy, become aware and to have the best life you can imagine. You are on earth to learn to create and there are no limits to what you can have! What you see in your outer world is a result of your inner world— the way you think, visualize, your beliefs, expectations, decisions, past programming, and ability to give and receive love.

"What is inside you at your deepest and highest levels is truly beautiful, and learning to bring that beauty into the world, into your environment, relationships, career, physical body, is part of the challenge of your earth experience."[10]

Although Orin encourages and offers guidance, he often steers clear of predictions. In fact, when Sanaya first started channeling, he *refused* to make predictions. At first the channel was disappointed, though Orin patiently explained that he did not want people coming for readings who just wanted to hear the future or to be told what to do.

However, after several years, Orin began to teach Sanaya about the future and probable realities. "Several times he gave me exact newspaper headlines and dates, several months prior to their occurring. All the predictions centered around mass events.

"He told me that large-scale events are easier to predict because they have energy lines from mass consciousness set up many months in advance. Whereas one person can change his mind and thus change his future easily."

In the future, it is likely that Sanaya Roman, her partner Duane Packer, and their company, Lumin-Essence Productions, will be ever more powerful in the channeling movement. With the aid of their spirit guides, they have published the best-selling *Opening to Channel: How to Connect with Your Guide*. Together they have taught hundreds of people to channel through their weekend channeling courses. The cost of the seminar, Opening to Channel, is $350 per person. Enrollment is limited, usually booked solid several months in advance, and the classes often take place in the San Francisco Bay area, where Roman and Packer make their home.

Sanaya has also produced a line of guided meditation tapes dictated by Orin, from "Being Happy," "Finding the Cause," "Visualizing and Energy Work" to "Developing a Thin Personality" and "Creating Your Own Body." Included in the LuminEssence tape catalogue is a listing of New Age music cassettes to help facilitate the channeling experience.

"My goal," says Orin, "is to assist you in making your earth life work, for through working in the spiritual realms, connecting with your soul, and calling in higher guidance, life can be joy, love and abundance. When you work with the higher energies of the universe, the practical, everyday issues can be handled with greater ease. You are a beautiful being, and I welcome you back to the higher levels of love and light that are your natural home."

Duane Packer/DaBen

Once you bring through a high-level guide, or connect with your soul self, you will be on an accelerated growth path. Opening to channel creates a greater link between the superconscious self and the ordinary self. This opening creates or accelerates a spiritual awakening. Your guides will be able to assist you with this awakening. They will help you experience more joy, more confidence, more awareness of who you are.

—Orin and DaBen[11]

Without Sanaya Roman and her spirit entity, Orin, Duane Packer might never have opened his channel to welcome in DaBen. But, as frequently is the case, Duane met Sanaya at a most auspicious moment in his life.

Duane began his career as a scientist with a Ph.D. in geology-geophysics, spending most of his day working in an office with other scientists. In the evenings, he pursued a career doing bodywork—an interest that developed because of his enthusiasm for running. The first few years of Duane's jogging produced some painful injuries in his ankles, feet and knees. "But I began to realize that I could fix my injuries by using my mind to change the way I thought about the injury, then restructuring the muscles through physical manipulation. I realized I could fix other people's injuries the same way," he wrote in *Opening to Channel*.

As Duane worked on a client's physical pain, he began to sense shifts in energy. He also felt a presence in the room, but kept rejecting the idea because of his scientific background. Around this time, a friend gave a special gift to Duane—a session with Sanaya and Orin. "The reading really made me reexamine the way I thought about my life, though I didn't believe Orin when he told me that I would probably quit my job, nor was I convinced that channeling was real."

Not too long after the reading, Duane began to have startlingly vivid psychic experiences. "One day as I was running in the hills, everything became moving patterns. The trees no longer looked like trees but like vibrational patterns and I could see right through them.

"A few days later, I pulled up alongside a car at a stoplight. I glanced over at a woman driver, and, to my shock, instead of seeing a person I saw a cocoon of light and energy lines all around her body."

Meanwhile, Duane continued to see Sanaya. Among other changes, his healing practice began to attract other channelers and those who were sensitive to psychic energy. His own psychic sensitivities increased and he was able to "distinguish three and then four qualities or layers of energy. Later, through close observation, I discovered these were closely linked with people's physical, mental, emotional and spiritual auras."

During this period Duane had another vivid psychic

incident. While he was driving, he seemed to hear a voice whispering the name "DaBen" in his ear. When Duane spent a full day in April of 1984 with Sanaya, Orin suggested he invite the presence named DaBen closer by speaking his name out loud. "I began to get hot and cold. I started seeing Sanaya in colors and layers, and I could see right through her. The entity seemed to come closer and become more real. The physical sensations were very strong, my lower diaphragm was vibrating uncontrollably and I was gasping for breath." Duane admits he probably needed this sort of dramatic introduction to DaBen because of his skeptical nature; now he connects with the entity much more easily.

As DaBen and Orin explain (they often channel cooperatively), "The entry of a high-level guide is almost always gentle, except in some rare cases when the vibration of the guide is dramatically different from yours. In our experiences and in those of the many people we have observed, guides would rather come to you so gently that you would doubt their presence rather than take the chance of worrying or frightening you. Because most guides enter gently, and most often your trance is light and your own consciousness is present, you may find yourself wondering: Is this my imagination?

"As you continue channeling you will be able to feel the vibratory presence of your guide as different from your own. Guides have a vibration beyond your normal range of perception, and it may take a while for you to distinguish between yourself and your guide."

As a result of what transpired that historic day in 1984, Duane decided to give up his career as an orthodox scientist and follow a path in bodywork, empowering others and channeling. From that decision, Sanaya and Duane started channeling together. Their guides appear to know each other, and their talks are often a collaborative effort.

Duane says, "I experience DaBen as a very radiant energy, loving and exacting, who has great caring. His knowledge is very detailed and intensive. Some of the information is so complex that he has been assisting me in developing new words to transmit it. He does not want me to gloss over his concepts or simplify them, even when people cannot immediately understand them. Often I have to consult my own physics books to understand what he might be explaining."

DaBen's scientific bent was certainly not coincidental. DaBen and Orin share the same reasons for entities choosing certain identities: "Guides will choose an identity that will best accomplish what they are here to do, or one that you can most relate to. There are as many identities for guides as there are for people, so be open to whatever form or appearance your guide presents him- or herself to you in. Some guides are purely intellectual and want to impart new ideas of science, logic, math or new systems of thought."

Along with DaBen, his scientific and healing entity, Duane is writing/channeling a book on human energy systems. He also teaches intuitive and advanced systems of bodywork to professionals and works with many therapists, doctors, chiropractors, athletes and healers. Duane also teaches classes in clairvoyant sight, and is active in most areas of the LuminEssence projects, including weekend intensives with Sanaya.

Tam Mossman/James

Actually, quite often, a channel brings through an entity which is in a way a creation assembled from the raw materials of the channel's unconscious. In other words, the entity gets the approval of the channel but on a quite intuitive basis. What you're speaking to now is a collaboration which has been worked through and refined over a period of several years.

—James

One afternoon in 1967, a manuscript came across the desk of an assistant editor at Prentice-Hall. The editor was Tam Mossman and the over-the-transom submission was from Jane Roberts. It was a sequel to the book *How to Develop Your ESP Powers*. Mossman recalls, "It was basically a manual on how somebody who had no experience in the field would be able to do ESP tests and get a Ouija board going. I read it over and then wrote back to Jane saying that I felt most of the material was pretty standard stuff but that the spirit guide, Seth, had an awful lot to say for himself. I asked her, 'What would happen if you wrote a book just about Seth?' "

The Seth material was published in 1970. "It did alright," says Mossman, "not super. I had contracted Jane to do a sequel to the Seth book anyway. I realized, like Cayce, you had to build up a collection." But for a number of reasons, the manuscript she wrote didn't progress enough to meet Mossman's satisfaction. "It didn't take the Seth concept and push it as far as I thought it needed to be pushed," Mossman says.

In the interim, he went to visit Jane and her husband, Rob, in their Elmira home. He learned during his visit that Seth was writing his own book. Mossman jokingly remarked, "Sorry, I can't offer you a contract but Jane is still working on her sequel." Seth said, "Oh, don't worry, it will get published."

Thanks to Mossman's foresight, the *Seth Speaks* classic did reach publication. But not without an element of conspiracy. Unbeknownst to anyone at Prentice-Hall, he substituted Seth's manucript for Roberts's. "The publishers to this day don't know what occurred. I don't mind if they find out now. All the people that could have fired me are no longer there."

In the fall of 1975, Tam Mossman had his own psychic breakthrough under the most unlikely circumstances. He was giving a presentation on Roberts's *The Nature of Personal Reality* to salesmen at a Catskill resort. "It was a rainy weekend, and I thought playfully, just to liven things up, I'll pretend that Seth has taken over my body." But what Mossman meant as a prank turned into a powerful and unforgettable experience. "When I began to do the Seth bit, I felt this great rush of energy—different from anything I had ever experienced before in my life."

The next time Mossman went to Elmira, he baited

Seth to see whether he knew that Tam had used his name in vain while at the meeting in the Catskills. Seth said simply, "It's not whether I can figure out what you did at the sales presentation, it's your responsibility to figure out where that energy came from."

By the summer of 1975, Mossman had begun to channel frequently. His entity calls himself James. The entity uses the analogy of the banyan tree to explain the vibrational level of his personality. The guide sends down various aerial roots to what we think of on our plane of physical reality as the ground. Mossman is one of those aerial roots.

Tam says the experience of channeling James is similar to the dream state. "I'm around, though like a dream, when I'm through, I forget what's happened. A little like waking from a nap, I feel mellow and a little woozy after having channeled.

"I can't demand that James arrive, but I can say no. Although there have been times when he's been really insistent because he wants to get a specific message through. It's been easier to just say at those times, 'To hell with it' . . . and let him through.

"But he's not the kind of entity who tries to do it for you. He doesn't say, 'Alright, kid, this is what it's all about.' He's more like a parent teaching a kid to walk. He'll put his hand out and make you do the actual intuition, reasoning and thinking," says Mossman.

James explains the reason for our readiness to be guided this way: "You have exhausted to a large degree your sense of wonder in the next mountain range, the next continent. Space did not open up quite as rapidly as some of your scientists foresaw. Again, when you find yourselves earthbound and feeling clustered and crowded and on an earth that is getting less and less natural each day, you are willing to reach out to the wonder, to the strangeness that takes you out of yourself. If nature is being denied that role, then you will search out the wonder, willy-nilly, in your own way, your own fashion."

James does not, however, like many guides, feel that the approaching millennium is necessarily responsible for the change in human readiness. "It is much easier for those who do not want to change overnight," explains James, "to look ahead at thirteen years and think, 'Good, I have a long time to get my act together.' But the change is going on even as we speak and a very dramatic change it is too."

Tam Mossman, meanwhile, caught up in the change, is very prominent within the channeling community. His respected journal, *Metapsychology*, is sold by subscription and in occult and New Age bookstores across the country. The journal focuses on the best transcribed material that channels and their entities have to offer as well as other areas of psychic interest. In the back of the magazine, James answers questions, many of which are submitted by the readers.

Mossman sees a future for the development of channeling: "The message in the future will be offered in a much more complex way. When we get the basics down, like creating our own realities, then we'll ask, 'Well, how do we do it?' Once we get the camel in the door," says Mossman, "then we'll work on getting the caravan in."

Ron Scolastico

In the beginning of earth, in the physical form as it does now show itself, there were certain conglomerations of forces that you could understand as a loose coalition of souls themselves. Therefore it would be similar to races, but separated not by the color of the body or the shape but by the intention. Therefore there would be races of wills. And many of these ones, for there were numerous ones, did choose to learn through trial and error. For their strength was very great. And these ones did choose to manifest in the physical form of the human.

—The Guides

One of the few trance mediums with a Ph.D., Dr. Ron Scolastico has been channeling the Guides for over a decade. During that time, he has given more than 9,000 readings. Ron's entities describe themselves as "advanced souls who have already evolved through a series of earth incarnations, and who now exist in a realm of beauty and love that lies beyond the physical world."

Ron, a former academic, began his journey with the Guides rather reluctantly. The first turning point in his life came just after completing his Ph.D. He was sitting in his office at the University of Iowa, thinking about his future and imagining landing a lucrative position at a prestigious university. The phone rang. Sure enough, it was the sort of offer that Scolastico coveted. But instead of rejoicing, he told the voice on the other end, "I want to thank you very much for your interest, but I'm seriously considering another offer, and I'm just not able to respond to yours right now."

At first Scolastico was astonished at his own words, but then he had a sudden realization. "I did *not* want to teach what my new Ph.D. qualified me to teach [an interdisciplinary study of humanistic psychology and human communication theory]. Even though at the conscious level I thought I was ready to take it on, my inner wisdom knew better, and it had come to my rescue just in time."

In what Scolastico calls "a rare burst of clarity and certainty" he understood that what he really wanted to do in his life was teach spiritual truths. He took a job working for minimum wage in a frame shop and in the evenings held an intellectual study group, teaching the principles of spiritual growth. But something was still very confusing and unsatisfying in Ron's life. He accepted a friend's suggestion to see a trance channel, hoping some of his confusion would be cleared.

On his way to the medium's house, on a cold winter's evening, he stopped to gaze at the sky. "While I stood staring at that brilliant moon, I started to feel a deep sense of expanded awareness. All at once, I was feeling acutely vital and alive. This was accompanied by an intense thrill of joy and exuberance that shot through my entire being; a kind of vibrant 'energy' coursed through and around me."

By the time Ron got to the channel's house, the experience of the moon had almost completely dissipated. He sat across from the channel, hugging his skepticism to his heart. However, the reading was so on target that even he was turned around. Over the following months, Ron continued to seek the guidance of channeled entities. During one session the voice said, "You have promised to be a trance medium in this lifetime." "My first thought," Ron remembers, "was, Wait a minute, you've got the wrong person!"

But on reconsidering, Ron felt that he had nothing to lose by giving it a try. After several months of aborted attempts, a guide with a thick Irish brogue began to speak through Ron. A decade later, the brogue is gone, but Scolastico has grown from a reluctant intellectual to a master channel.

The messages of his Guides are expressed with love. Ron leaves his body while he channels, but that "space" is filled with intense love. So strong is this emotion during sessions that many times his clients burst into tears of joy at the end of a reading, often exclaiming that they have never before felt so unconditionally loved.

The Guides explain, in their sometimes obtuse fasion, that many of us have a limited understanding of the meaning of love. "First is the emotion, then the power, the force that would be understood by yourself, perhaps, as nature, as the force that would cause growth and change and natural movement. Then beyond this would be the understanding of this force as a seed, an impregnation force."

The subject that is most important to explore, feels Scolastico, "is the area of spiritual truth—the knowledge about our souls and their place in the universe. For those who have come seeking truth and spiritual guidance, the readings have provided an apparently unlimited source of knowledge and inspiration."

For added inspiration, Scolastico's wife, Susan, helps Ron with the more material aspects of his channeling endeavors. Together they share a home, with Susan's daughter, in the Pacific Palisades on California's southern coast. Scolastico holds private and group sessions at his home and across the country. He also conducts a five-day spiritual retreat with Susan and the Guides at the Serra Retreat Center, founded in the 1940s by the Franciscan friars. The cost, including room and board, is $800.

Audio tapes of the Guides are also available on subjects such as the nature of loving, maintaining physical health, experiencing God, as well as dozens of other topics. Scolastico says about the Guides' recorded words: "In a deeply loving way, the spoken words of the Guides create an intense focus of spiritual attunement that helps the listener penetrate deeper levels of truth."

Ruth Montgomery

The earth is passing Universal Truth. It is awakening people to the reality of one world, one Creator, one Universal Truth—the eternal truth that there is no death and that love is the unifying force of the cosmic world. Such an attitude will help human beings to overcome their fears and reach out with helpfulness to others when the earth undergoes periods of famine, flood, earthquakes, and spasmodic warfare.

—The Guides[12]

Ruth Montgomery is considered by many to be the First Lady of psychic writing. For the past quarter century she has devoted her career and her personal life to understanding the mysteries of our existence. She is the author of fourteen books—ten of which explore worlds beyond our five senses. Thanks to Ruth Montgomery and her Guides, the ideas of reincarnation, UFOs, channeling, automatic writing, life on other spheres and the coming of the New Age have been made available to millions of readers. The Guides made it clear to Ruth from the start of their contact that their purpose in communicating with her was not to serve as a medium for individual contact, but to share information affecting all mankind.

Montgomery began her writing career as a journalist covering the Washington political scene. "I was a newspaper reporter, as skeptical as the average member of my profession," she wrote in her autobiography, *Herald of the New Age.* "We have covered too many political huddles in smoke-filled rooms and exposed too many chicaneries to believe all that meets the eye. But a good reporter must also have an open mind."[13]

Indeed, the most prominent aspects of Ruth's nature are her openness to any possibility (no matter how seemingly farfetched) and her curiosity. It was probably these qualities that led her to accept her sister-in-law Rhoda's invitation to attend a séance while Ruth and her husband, Bob, were visiting St. Petersburg, Florida, in 1956. The reporter was impressed with the medium, Dr. Malcolm Pantin. After the séance, she asked him whether he knew of any mediums in Washington. Montgomery's curiosity had been piqued and she wanted to investigate further.

On her return to the D.C. area, Montgomery began visiting the psychics on Pantin's list. She described all her experiences in a series on psychics and séances for her syndicated column. After months of research, she was still not totally convinced that all the mediums she had interviewed were aboveboard. At the conclusion of her series of articles, she printed a command directed to spirits: "The next move," she wrote, "is up to them!"

But there was one medium with whom she felt an immediate affinity—Arthur Ford. She asked what he thought about Ouija boards. Ford sat quietly for a moment, then answered: "Well, some people have been successful in discovering psychic ability that way, but it should not be used as a party plaything, because it can also be dangerous if the wrong type of entities are attracted. I'll go into trance and you can see what Fletcher [Ford's spirit entity] has to say. Then you can form your own judgment."[14]

But when Ford went into a trance, Fletcher did not discuss the Ouija board. Instead he gave messages from the beyond from people who, Ruth later verified, were old friends and relatives of her husband, Bob. All were deceased.

After this encounter, Arthur Ford continued to play an important role in Montgomery's psychic development. "I'm getting vibrations that you have the talent to develop automatic writing ability and I wish you would try," Ford encouraged.

Montgomery took Ford's suggestion to heart. Every single day, at the same time, she ran through a special program: head and neck exercises, a mantra, meditation and a silent prayer for protection. Then she held her pen poised. Finally, after months of what seemed like futile attempts, her pen began automatically to make large, flowing figure eights. She was starting on the road that would change her life.

One morning, using her automatic hand, the symbol of a delicate lily appeared. The writing announced, "This is the identification by which you will know, each morning from now on, that it is I who is coming through."[15] Montgomery said of her initial experiences with Lily, "From that time on, every single day the pencil drew the flower and wrote 'Lily', then began the most beautiful philosophy that I had ever read. I knew that it wasn't coming from me. I had never had such inspiring thoughts in my whole life."

Lily gave indications of what Montgomery was to meet in her future. Lily also suggested vehemently that she give up smoking, cocktails, tea, Cokes, chocolate . . . "anything harmful to the body." Montgomery's feisty reaction was, "Wait a minute! Whose life is this, anyway?" (She did give up smoking and cocktails.)

Ruth's morning sessions began to grow in speed and strength until she received a message to work from her typewriter rather than with a pad and pen. Sure enough, once she placed her fingers gently on the keys, they began to tap nonstop.

Lily was replaced by spirits who identified themselves merely as the Guides, and they assured Montgomery that the knowledge and truth she was gaining was in great need of being shared with the rest of humankind. But Montgomery was still very much involved with her political writing in Washington, and hesitated to "go out in the open" with the Guides' messages, no matter how important and clarifying they were.

"The very thought that thinking human beings sprang fully developed in that one state of existence would seem laughable to any except you earth people, who are accustomed to accepting everything at face value," the Guides wrote.[16] "You who are more advanced and sensitive have lived through many previous phases, while some of your more doltish varieties had only primer training in a previous stop. To that life which went before, you are as much the 'hereafter' as we are to you.

"The hereafter goes on and on, my dear child, until at last you and we and all of us eventually pass through that Golden Door where longing shall be no more, where perfection has been attained, and where we are at last one with God, our Creator."[17]

Ruth kept filing the Guides' messages in a drawer. But after her huge success with the book *A Gift of Prophecy*, the story of the psychic Jeane Dixon, Montgomery decided to write the book her Guides had been dictating—*A Search for the Truth*. It recounted her ten-year journey into the realm of psychic exploration, and became a best-seller in a matter of weeks.

With that success, Montgomery began her series of psychic publications, all dictated by the Guides through automatic writing. Her next book was titled *Here and Hereafter*, which told the story of her own hypnotic regression back to past lives as well as the experiences of others. Of course, it contained a tremendous amount of information passed along by the Guides. She also received considerable help and encouragement from the nutritionist Adelle Davis, whom she disguised in the book, but whose identity she revealed after Davis's death.

"It's not overly important whether we 'believe in reincarnation,' " Montgomery wrote at the close of her book. "If the laws of karma and grace are real, they will survive without our attestation. What does matter is that we conduct ourselves in such manner that we incur no bad karmic indebtedness. The skeptic may ask, 'What if there's no such thing as karma or reincarnation, or eternal life?' " To which Montgomery answers, "What if there is?"

She channeled her next book, *A World Beyond*, with Arthur Ford, who had passed on during the previous year. Ford's messages from the beyond were filled with deep and passionate knowledge. "God," he explained, "is the core of the universe from which all else flows forth. He is truth and energy. He is matter and spirit, and all things of heaven and earth. He is also the essence of our being, without which nothing would exist ... God is! The eternal I AM."[18]

Ford, from the beyond, encouraged Ruth to spread the message. "We are the co-creators with God of what we find for ourselves here," he said. "Ruth, we want you to wake the people up to the importance of this towering truth."[19]

After the success of *A World Beyond*, Ruth continued to explore and answer other questions concerning man's existence. Her books *Companions Along the Way*, *The World Before*, *Strangers Among Us* and *Threshold to Tomorrow* explored with thorough documentation, true to Montgomery's journalistic style, the phenomena of walk-ins, aliens, channels and their spirits, as well as the origins of the earth, souls and a glimpse into our future.

Ruth's Guides foretell what lies ahead. They predict that the earth will tilt over on its axis, the oceans will overflow, the earth will open. There will reign every conceivable natural catastrophe. Yet, we will somehow evolve from our necessary and unavoidable misfortunes. The Guides explain, "The New Age is the crossover from the present mundane world of the body and its comforts to the spiritual plane and its reality of one world, on one universe, one cosmos. This period will last for the biblical thousand years of peace and brotherhood, when men's minds will be opened to each other and to the forces beyond earth's own magnetic center."[20]

During her decade-long investigations into the spirit world, Montgomery has remained totally convinced that "the spirit plane is as real as the physical world that we can see and touch, and that communication with that world indeed exists." For many thousands of devoted and grateful readers, Montgomery is a master at that communication.

Branda Carl/Myrios

To better understand your "creation,"
you need better understand its creator.
The "you" creating your life is not limited to the individual living it but is the
sum total of all the "Yous" you have
ever been or will ever be. The creative
you is the greater you, the higher you:
your higher self.

—Myrios

Branda Carl walked away from a fourteen-year career
as a social worker with Chicago's Department of Public Aid and onto a spiritual path, becoming one of the
city's most active channeling organizers. Her psychic
networking efforts, she hopes, will result in a more
unified New Age community. "I am working with other
New Age metaphysical practitioners to establish a
school/healing center," she explains. "I would like to
provide a source center where people can obtain quality service, as well as a place where those providing
these services can learn new techniques in a suppor-
tive setting.

"As much as we say we are one, the Chicago New

Age community is not all that together. Spirituality has little to do with bean sprout consumption nor is it simply saying the right things. One has to feel them— to live them."

Myrios, the entity who speaks from Branda, accesses through a trance state, the depth and level of trance determining the voice and quality of the information communicated. Myrios defines himself as a "healing-teaching collective composed of energy intelligence that exists on a number of planes concurrently." The level of information transmitted is dependent on Branda's own energy. "If I'm resonating at a lower frequency, I'm receiving lower level information. I am 'told' I have not yet accessed Myrios at the level I will eventually achieve."

Before the energy enters Branda she sees a spray of indigo blue lights followed by a luminous violet sphere that grows larger as it approaches. "Once this happens, I'm out," she says. She is often unaware of the channeled messages, unless "the information being channeled is a generic lesson with overall application—or it is one of my own lessons."

Branda feels that Myrios either ingests energy or simply adjusts the energy level vibrationally. In either case, she claims Myrios is responsible for numerous electrical calamities. Most recently, while Myrios and Branda were guests on a Chicago radio program, the telephones were temporarily knocked out of service. "Nothing permanent. They 'healed' when I calmed down." Still, she refers to herself as a "sort of Typhoid Mary when it comes to electrical appliances." (A similar episode occurred to Susan Chicovsky, the Colorado channel, while being interviewed on a nationally syndicated radio program.)

Myrios's sessions are either thirty or sixty minutes long, and Branda supplies a tape for no additional fee.

She does not duplicate tapes, so that complete confidentiality is assured. During the course of a reading, Myrios frequently suggests to clients that they listen to Lazaris's material. "He says that it brings people up nicely," reports Branda, "but I do not mean to suggest Myrios is Lazaris or in any way connected to Lazaris, only that the material is complementary. Myrios has also recommended other books, techniques and local healers.

"Essentially, Myrios provides insight that enables an individual to better understand why certain events occur. Understanding why we do the things we do empowers us to change our behavior so we can better begin to consciously create more satisfying lives. The more we understand ourselves, the more we can act rather than react. Myrios helps us to do this," says the channel.

Myrios assures us that we are not alone, that though we are separate we are more similar than different, and that our spirits and energy are eternal: "Man looks for eternal life not realizing he already has it. What would be the purpose of existing eternally in one body when one body can provide you only one limited perspective? The American Indians say you must walk in another man's moccasins to truly know him. You have walked in a variety of footwear—that is what allows you the understanding of each other—that is why your energy remains intact. Though you have the illusion of being separate, you are very much the same energy. You are not all in it together; you are it together."

The entity/energy, like most other spirit guides, is firm in his message that we create our own reality and are totally responsible for our own lives. "That winning lottery ticket will never come to you as long

as you believe, at a feeling level, rewards on the physical plane must be earned. As long as you believe you
are less than perfect, you will continue to create romances, jobs and life experiences that are less than
perfect. You create for yourself the life you feel you
deserve."

Darryl Anka/Bashar

Any individuals who can magnetically align and center themselves within the blue-white electromagnetical field of your planet, in that blended and balanced state, what might be called the idealized blueprint state, cannot, by definition, contain any disease of any nature at all.

—Bashar

What sets Darryl Anka apart from numerous other California channelers who communicate with spirit guides is that Anka claims to be in touch with Bashar, an extraterrestrial from the Orion constellation. His first contact with the outerplanetary came thirteen years ago, when he was in his early twenties: "On two different occasions within the span of the same week, with four friends the first time, and two friends present the second time, we had close, broad daylight, physical sighting of Bashar's spacecraft over Los Angeles," Darryl reports.

Spurred by the sighting, Anka began to read and study all he could find on a wide variety of metaphysical subjects. He developed a particularly sharp interest in mediumship and introduced himself to several channelers. Eventually Bashar and his peers made a mental connection with Anka. As soon as the link was formed, Darryl reports remembering that in a past life he had made a pact with the aliens to act as their medium.

"The memory of having made the agreement came back: Who they were, who I was to them, what the ship sighting had been for, dream encounters I'd had with them that I'd totally blocked up to that point—they all came back in that one memory as well."

Bashar then sent his first telepathic message: "Okay, now is the time for you to start doing this if you still want to. Do you still want to?" Darryl answered in the affirmative.

Anka learned that Bashar, who exists in a telepathic society, chose his name so that Anka would have a reference point—something to call him. Bashar selected the word from the Arabic since that is the channel's heritage. The word means "commander," which is similar to his position in his planetary society. It also means "the being" or "the man." In Armenian, *Bashar* simply means "the messenger."

Many of Bashar's messages are lessons to help earth's people understand their existence. "Synchronicity is your conscious recognition that all the objects, all the relationships, all points of view, all perceptions, interactions—are all *one* thing. Every single thing that you experience, every differentiation that you create in your reality is the same one thing from a different point of view. The same *one* thing manifesting itself simultaneously as the illusion of many things."

Anka has "seen" Bashar and other extraterrestrials in his dreams: "The beings are somewhat Eurasian in feature, with enlarged eyes. They average about five feet in height and have whitish-gray skin color. The females usually have white hair, while the males have no hair. They are from Essasani (it means "Place of Living Light" in their older, nontelepathic language), which is approximately 500 light-years in the direction of the Orion constellation.

"But since they exist in a different vibrational plane from us," Anka explains, "their star is not visible."

Before channeling became his means of support, Darryl worked as a prop and special effects designer. Now he devotes his days and evenings to picking up Bashar's messages and passing them on either during private readings or with groups.

Paul Norris McClain

The orientation you now have with the
world is a fixed and set experience in
your mind. It is strangely interesting that
in order to know the self, there is the
need first to disorient yourself of it.

—Spirit Guide

"I steer clear of the spiritual and psychic community," explains one of Florida's busiest channels, thirty-
two-year-old Paul McClain. Though McClain has seen
thousands of clients in his Miami home and across
the country, channeled hundreds of guides and spends
most of his day in a deep trance, he is leery of what
he calls a recent wave of "spiritual fascism"—the belief that there is only one way to gather guidance from
the beyond.

McClain, in keeping with his earthly personality,
remembers that he was "skeptical, naive and reluctant" when he first began to communicate with spirit
guides. "Frequently, in the evenings when I would try
to fall asleep, I would come out of my body and hear
voices. It was especially frightening when I realized

that I was falling into a trance. I assumed I was going crazy, that it was some kind of schizophrenia."

Paul, who was living in New York City at the time, was on his way to Bellevue Hospital when fate intervened. Coincidentally, he met an old friend he hadn't seen for some time. "When I told her what was happening to me, she didn't seem surprised. She suggested, sort of offhandedly, that it might have something to do with a past life and recommended I see Alex Murray." Skeptical but desperate, Paul took her advice and saw Murray the next day.

"Frankly, I thought I was wasting my time, but then, while Alex was in a trance, one of the voices that had been trying to reach me came through *him*. My first reaction was utter astonishment. My second was relief; I realized I wasn't going mad.

"Once I calmed down, the voice asked if I wanted to do trance mediumship. I was emphatic. 'No!' I said. 'Absolutely not!' At the time, seven years ago, all I could think about was *The Exorcist*. To tell you the truth, I was just plain frightened. Because of my fear, I think the voices stopped for a period of time."

But despite his resistance, McClain gradually began to study under the tutelage of Murray and learned how to control his trances. He practiced making his physical entity available to spirits only during certain scheduled times. Now McClain spends most of his days in deep trance, channeling for a steady stream of clients who either come to his home or invite him to lecture and hold sessions in their area. (McClain is on the road approximately one third of the year.)

McClain's trances are exceptionally deep. While in a trance, Paul is not aware of an entity's message to a client. He does, however, hear his own guide on occasion. As a result, during his waking hours, he has developed very little of the spiritual affectation or jargon that often accompanies some channels' personalities. He does not presume to be highly developed or evolved.

"I fall asleep completely and have no memory of what happens while I'm in a trance. The reaction of other people after they've had a session—the way they look at me—leaves me a little stunned," he says. "At the beginning I used to worry that the information being passed on wasn't correct, but now I trust the guides.

"After channeling, I feel more energy and I feel healed emotionally and physically. That's probably why I've grown to trust them. If at any time I felt negative energy I would stop channeling immediately," he says.

McClain specializes in channeling personal, individual guides for his clients. He explains that about a third of the guides that come through are recognizable—the same ones that come to his mentor, Murray, while dozens of others he can't identify. (He sometimes listens to the tapes after sessions, though he doesn't make a practice of it.)

There are two basic messages that McClain's entities stress: "Getting in touch with yourself, your own power. They don't want people to rely on channelers. They want people to get in touch with them directly, to open their own psychic self.

"The other message that is fairly persistent is that people should feel their own unlimited energy and love. The spirits are always stressing unconditional love for yourself and others."

McClain's guides stay away from "fortune tellings" and focus instead on teaching. "The purpose of my individual readings," says McClain, "is to help clients get over their personal blocks. So, in the beginning, I'll do a reading to enable them to get in touch with their higher energy." But he warns, "The guides won't come through if they feel a person is too dependent."

The Miami channel also holds group classes emphasizing self-channeling. McClain believes strongly that anyone can learn to channel. "Some people receive inspiration and translate it, others get information that is broadcast loud and clear from an entity and they pick it up as though they are a receiving station. Sometimes, the entity comes into the body and replaces the soul completely. But communication with the beyond is always different. It's purely individual."

Shawn Randall/Torah

As you consciously take this endeavor to heart you are consciously choosing to grow in a very big way. You are consciously choosing to get more in touch with God/Goddess/All That Is, for the closer you can get to a guide or counselor around you that you might wish to channel, the closer you will be to All That Is.

—Torah

Five years ago, Shawn Randall was suffering writer's block. To work it through, she joined a class in mediumship taught by Los Angeles channel Thomas Jacobson. Toward the culmination of the course, while meditating, she began to experience stunning sensations in her heart and head. Utilizing the process of automatic writing, she asked what was going on. The answer was relayed clearly: Shawn Randall was being prepared to become a channel. She felt a wonderful rush of light and love and suddenly, out came the voice of an entity who identified herself as Martha. Soon to follow came the entity Charles and, two weeks later, Torah, who has remained Shawn's guide to this day.

Shawn explains, "Torah simply describes himself as 'interdimensional consciousness.' He says he is no longer incarnating, and he does not take on any characteristics or personality traits of any of his past lives. The information and the love he comes to share speaks for itself."

It takes the channel approximately one minute to ready herself for Torah, and she remains in a semi-conscious state while in communication with the entity. "I feel as if I am in a dream that moves on without my participation. I can hear Torah's words if I choose to, or move farther back into the comfortable sensations and not be aware. I experience pictures sometimes—energy patterns that somehow correlate with what Torah is saying.

"I also see past lives Torah may be describing to individuals who are wishing to use that kind of information as a tool for understanding themselves. When I come out of my altered state after channeling, I feel wonderful—never drained or depleted in any way."

Randall views channeling in psychological terms, as an evolution of consciousness. "In the past, Freud discovered the subconscious and its impact and influence on our lives; today we are exploring our superconscious, 'higher consciousness,' going beyond our subconscious. Channeling," she continues, "is the discovery of how to integrate other levels of consciousness into our daily lives."

Shawn began teaching people to channel two years ago. At first it was just at the request of close friends, but soon the requests mushroomed and now Randall holds six classes a week. She feels confident that though one can't be taught to be an "unconscious channel" (because this sort of channeling is arranged prior to a present lifetime), anybody with the desire can learn to be a conscious channel.

Torah agrees: "The key, of course, is the willingness, the openness, and the awareness that you are opening to being loved. So this is important. We would ask you to look at yourself and ask how willing do you feel to receive love in your life? For, if you are willing to receive love in all areas of your life, then the channeling process can work very quickly for you.

"But if you are feeling that channeling is going to be *the* source for you, the panacea that is going to completely change your valuing of yourself, or give you a sense of self-value that you never had before—well, think again because the guides tend to come to individuals who value themselves already, who are centered enough, who, in a sense, don't want to be told what to do, because the guides don't want to tell you what to do but rather assist you in seeing how to find the answers for yourself."

Classes are guided half by Torah, the other half by a totally conscious Shawn. They teach channeling as a twelve-week course, answering all questions and progressing step-by-step. In addition to her weekly classes, Randall channels larger public groups once a week. Extremely articulate about her work, Randall has channeled on radio shows, appeared on cable television, numerous network news broadcasts including CBS's *West 57th Street*, and writes regularly for New Age periodicals.

The message Torah and Shawn stress in their writings is self-reliance and personal responsibility. "The more you look at your life," says Torah, "the more you'll be able to open to channeling. The more responsibility you take for your life, the more responsibility you'll be able to take in your channeling, and the more will come to you as a result of it. . . . Very exciting."

Part
THREE

The New Age
Channeling Directory

The New Age Channeling Directory includes information culled from newsletter classifieds, newspaper and magazine articles, workshop directories, New Age bookstores, organization lecture series listings, channelers' recommendations, even signs posted in health-food stores. Inclusion in the directory is in no manner an endorsement; in several instances, I had little or no contact with the channelers or organizations listed.

In states such as California, New York and Illinois, where channeling has now become a major psychic activity, there are numerous entries. On the other hand, in some areas of the country channeling has not yet taken hold, or if it has, it is still very much an underground activity and channelers in these areas have declined to be identified.

Although every attempt was made to contact all those who are contributing to the New Age movement, I am certain that many have been omitted. To these pioneers, my apologies. Also, despite every effort to assure the currency and accuracy of the entries, due to recent moves and other changes, some errors (although I hope few), are possible.

A listing of Canadian channelers and services will be found at the end of the state-by-state directory.

KEY

A	Audio tape
B	Bookstore
C	Channeler
D	Directory
G	Group classes or workshops
M	Magazine
MP	Media production company specializing in taping both audio and video channeling sessions
N	Newsletter
O	Organization
P	Publication
R	Retreat where room and board are offered along with channeling seminars and workshops
S	Seminar
V	Video tape

ALABAMA

Channelers

Lisa McCombs
P.O. Box 55971
Birmingham, Alabama 35205
A C G P

Proes and Serena
3507 West Lakeside Drive
Birmingham, Alabama 35243
A C G P V

Services

Lodestar Books
2020 11th Avenue
Birmingham, Alabama 35205
A B G V

ALASKA

Channelers

Michael Francis
216 East 53rd
Anchorage, Alaska 99518
A C

Services

The A.T.O.M. Center
216 East 53rd
Anchorage, Alaska 99518
O

The Source
329 East Fifth Avenue
Cordova, Alaska 99501
A B V

Unicorn
9310 Glacier Highway

Juneau, Alaska 99801
A B

ARIZONA

Channelers

Dr. Frank Alper
Arizona Metaphysical Society
3939 E. Clarendon Road
Phoenix, Arizona 85018
A C G P S V

Jon-Terrence Diegel
Patricia-Rochelle
Church of Malabar
West Highway 89A   Suite 333
Sedona, Arizona 86336
A C G S

Myrna Ka Lange
Sunstar Press
Box 1901
Prescott, Arizona 86302
C

Jane Martin
Box 1389
Bisbee, Arizona 85603
C

Janet McClure
The Tibetan Foundation
12600 113th Avenue
Valley View Plaza   Suite #C19
Youngstown, Arizona 85363
A C G S

Barbara Morlan
Universal Rainbow Center
118 Thelma Drive
Prescott, Arizona 86301
A C G P S

Margaret M. Myers
Universarium Foundation
P.O. Box 890
Taylor, Arizona 85939
C G P S

Jason Peterson
c/o Gina Vareli
Metaphysical Consultants
P.O. Box 64027
Tucson, Arizona 85603
A C

Pete A. Sanders, Jr.
Free Soul
P.O. Box 1762
Sedona, Arizona 86336
A C G S

NA Scott
2675 West Highway 89A
Suite 130
Sedona, Arizona 86336
C

Services

Alpha
1928 E. McDowell
Phoenix, Arizona 85006
A B

Aradia
116 West Cottage
P.O. Box 266
Flagstaff, Arizona 85018
A B

A.R.E.
4018 N. 40th Street
Phoenix, Arizona 85018
O

Arizona Metaphysical Society
3939 E. Clarendon Road
Phoenix, Arizona 85018

A P S V

Church of Malabar
2675 West Highway 89A
Suite 333
Sedona, Arizona 86336
N O

Cradle of the Sun
Box 616
Route 179
Sedona, Arizona 86336
O

Dimensions
Box 211
Rimrock, Arizona 86335
M

Free Soul
P.O. Box 1762
Sedona, Arizona 86336
A N O S

Golden Word
3150 West Highway 89A
P.O. Box 1953
Sedona, Arizona 86336
A B G V

Institute of Metapsychology
2675 West Highway 89A
Suite 333
Sedona, Arizona 86336
O

Light Unlimited
4747 E. Thomas Road
Phoenix, Arizona 85018
A B

Omega
6418 S. 39th Avenue
Phoenix, Arizona 85041
D

The New Age Study of
  Humanity's Purpose
P.O. Box 41883
Tucson, Arizona 85717
O

Sunstar Press
Box 1901
Prescott, Arizona 86302
P

The Tibetan Foundation
12600 113th Avenue
Valley View Plaza   Suite #C19
Youngstown, Arizona 85363
O S

Universal Rainbow Light Center
118 Thelma Drive
Prescott, Arizona 86301
P S

Universarium Foundation
P.O. Box 890
Taylor, Arizona 85939
P S

ARKANSAS

Channelers

Kathleen Douglass
SRA Box 451
Willow, Arkansas 99688
A C

Genieve Paulson
Dimensions of Evolvement
S.R. 3 Box 47
Melbourne, Arkansas 72556
C G P

Services

Dimensions of Evolvement
S.R. 3 Box 47
Melbourne, Arkansas 72556
P S

ESP Research Associates
  Foundation
Union National Plaza
Suite 1660
Little Rock, Arkansas 72201
N O

CALIFORNIA

Channelers

Gerri Allen
P.O. Box 1385
Westwood, California 96137
C N

Hilary Anderson, Ph.D.
P.O. Box 10261
Beverly Hills, California 90213
C

Darryl Anka
8371 Balboa Blvd. #30
Northridge, California 91325
A C G S

Rev. Barbara Bartole
1221 North Orange Street
La Habre, California 90631
A C G

Gerry Bowman
The Freewill Foundation
7210 Jordan Avenue D-23
Canoga Park, California 91304
C

Judy Brackett
4216 Beverly Blvd. Suite 240

Los Angeles, California 90004
C

Rama Das
P.O. Box 31131
San Francisco, California 94131
A C S

Susan Ford
Box 74872
Los Angeles, California 90004
C

Jennie Galuppo
"Messengers of Light"
P.O. Box 1158
Agoura Hills, California 91302
A C N V

Richard L. Greer
Box 44
2550 Shattuck Avenue
Berkeley, California 94704
A C G

Stephen D. Hewitt
3915 Prospect Avenue
Los Angeles, California
A C G

Thomas Jacobson
2721 Via Anita
Palos Verdes Estate, California
   90274
A C G S

Jacqueline
Triune Light Center
1201 Wilshire Blvd #254
West Los Angeles, California
   90025
C

Michael Kant
2527 Niles Street #1

Bakersfield, California 93306
C G S

Karen
Box 942
Bellflower, California 90706
C

Connie Komisar
Generic Psychic
2137 Penny Lane
Napa, California 94559
C G

Tayrn Krive
P.O. Box 6026–425
Sherman Oaks, California 91413
A C G

Jack Levic
P.O. Box 93813
Los Angeles, California 90093
A C N

Bruce E. MacRae
1236 Pacific Avenue #3
Los Angeles, California 90066
C G

Thomas P. Massari
Genesis Reflection
P.O. Box 4111
Simi Valley, California 93063
A C G V

Sue Maywald
Channeled Bodywork
6615 Whitney Street
Oakland, California 94559
C

Duane Packer
LuminEssence
P.O. Box 19117
Oakland, California 94619
A C N P

Jach Pursel
Concept: Synergy
279 South Beverly Drive
Suite 604
Los Angeles, California 90212
A C G S V

Azana Ramada
Reflections of Divinity
P.O. Box 30724
Santa Barbara, California 93130
A C G S V

Shawn Randall
4220 Colfax
Studio City, California 91604
A C G V

David Rapkin, Ph.D.
3122 Santa Monica Blvd. P.H.
   West
Santa Monica, California 90404
A C G

Andrew Reiss
2314-6 Glendale Blvd.
Los Angeles, California 90039
A C G N

Sanaya Roman
LuminEssence
P.O. Box 19117
Oakland, California 94619
A C N P

Neville Rowe
7985 Santa Monica Blvd. #109/
   223
West Hollywood, California
   90046
A C N

Lyssa Royal
8585 Melrose Avenue
Los Angeles, California 90069
A C

Kevin Ryerson
3315 Sacramento Street
Suite #339
San Francisco, California 94118
A C G

Ron Scolastico, Ph.D.
P.O. Box 1302
Pacific Palisades, California
   94118
C G R

Oh Shinnah
Four Directions Foundation
632 Oak Street
San Francisco, California 94117
C G S

Dick Sutphen
Box 38
Malibu, California 90265
A C P S

Diane Tessman
P.O. Box 622
Poway, California 92064
C

Penny Torres
P.O. Box 20904
Vacaville, California 95696
C G

Stephen and April White
2899 Agoura Road   Suite 193
Westlake Village, California
   91361
A C G N

Services

American Parapsychological
Research Foundation
Box 8447
Calabasas, California 91302
O S

Aquarius Ranch
  Communications
11020 Ventura Blvd.
Studio City, California 91604
N

Association for Love and Light
8585 Melrose Avenue
Los Angeles, California 90069
M P

Astral Publishing
428 Coronado Avenue   #7
Long Beach, California 90814
M

Blue Mountain Center
330 E. Canon Perdido Street
Santa Barbara, California 93101
S

Bodhi Tree
8585 Melrose Avenue
Los Angeles, California 90291
B D

California Miracles Center
612 Clayton Suite 5
San Francisico, California 94117
N O

The Clairvoyant
Box 39
2550 Shattuck Avenue
Berkeley, California 94704
M

Concept: Synergy
Lazaris
279 South Beverly Drive
Suite 604
Los Angeles, California 90212
A O P S V

The Consciousness Connection
432 Altair Place

Venice, California 90291
M

Dolphin Dreams Newsletter
2272 Colorado Blvd.   #1125–G
Los Angeles, California 90041
N

Dolphin Perspective
428 Coronado Avenue   #7
Long Beach, California 90814
A P S
(excursions)

Foundation for Inner Peace
Course in Miracles
P.O. Box 635
Tiburon, California 94920
A N O P V

Four Directions Foundation
632 Oak Street
San Francisco, California 94117
G O S

Gathering of Affinity and Light
(G.O.A.L.)
428 Coronado Avenue   #7
Long Beach, California 90814
G O

The Healix Center
Bette-Barr Glover, Director
23732 Birtcher Street
El Toro, California 92630
A B G N P

Inner Joy
628 South Harbor Blvd.   # 347
Santa Ana, California 92704
D

Inner Light Foundation
P.O. Box 761
Novato, California 94948
N O

The Institute of Psychic
  Development
2521 Dana Street
Berkeley, California 94704
O S

J & S Aquarian Networking
Joshua Shapiro and Sharon
  Bowen
Pinole, California 94564
D N

Life Times
P.O. Box 4129
Santa Barbara, California 93140
M

The Light Connection
P.O. Box 1085
Cardiff, California 92007
N

LuminEssence
P.O. Box 19117
Oakland, California 94619
A N P.

Messages from Michael
11 Sir Francis Drake Blvd.
Suite 3C141
Greenboro, California 94904
N
(the only Michael material
  authorized by Chelsea
  Quinn Yarbro)

National New Age Yellow Pages
P.O. Box 5491
Fullerton, California 92635
D

New Era Media
Visual Music for Meditations
P.O. Box 410685
San Francisco, California 94141
A MP V

Penny Price Productions
Complete Guide to Channeling
7270 Hillside Street
Los Angeles, California 90046
A P V

Psychic Research Inc.
Marcel Vogel, Ph.D.
1725 Little Orchard Street
San Jose, California 95125
N O

Right and Happy Productions
17 Ardor Drive
Orina, California 94563
MP N

Seminars w' Seth
4634 Briggs
La Crescenta, California 91214
O

Spectrum Communication
10616 Moor Park Avenue
Toluka Lake, California 91602
MP

Spirit Speaks
P.O. Box 84304
Los Angeles, California 90073
M P S

Spiritual Emergence Network
250 Oak Grove Avenue
Menlo Park, California 94025
G N O S

Unity-and-Diversity World
  Organization
1010 S. Flower Street
Suite 500
Los Angeles, California 90015
A N P

Valley of the Sun Publishing
Box 38

Malibu, California 90265
P

VOICE
Asatara
P.O. Box 5003
800 W. Arrow Highway
Upland, California 91786
N O

COLORADO

Channelers

Joy Ballas
Certified Hypnotist
P.O. Box 9002   #375
Boulder, Colorado 80301
A C G

Susan Chicovsky
6569 South Keim Road
Evergreen, Colorado 80439
A C G S

John Cloonan
Certified Channel by
The Tibetan Foundation
6912 Millbrook Lane
Fountain, Colorado 80303
A C G

Beverly Criswell
Lavender Lines
P.O. Box 1090
Cripple Creek, Colorado 80813
A C G P S

Divya Degard
Certified Channel by
The Tibetan Foundation
137 31st Street
Boulder, Colorado 80204
A C G

Elaine Jay Finster
3826 South Yosemite
Denver, Colorado 80237
C G P S

Gurudas
P.O. Box 228
Boulder, Colorado 80306
A C G P S

Gail Joy Hoag
Metaforms
P.O. Box 2252
Boulder, Colorado 80306
C G

Gregory Jay
Metaforms
P.O. Box 2252
Boulder, Colorado 80306
C G

Kathryn Kingdon
c/o Susan Gordon, Manager
111154
Aurora, Colorado 80011
A C G S

Myron MacClellan
3917 South Fox
Englewood, Colorado 80110
A C

Diane Maria
P.O. Box 12134
12162 East Mississippi Av-
nue
Aurora, Colorado 80012
A C G S

Katie Marks
Transpersonal Counselor
P.O. Box 1425
Boulder, Colorado 80306
C G

Marsha Pac
Certified Channel by
The Tibetan Foundation
146 West Fifth Avenue
Denver, Colorado 80204
A C G

John and Alayna Rea
1272 Bear Mountain Court
Boulder, Colorado 80303
C G P S

Barbara Rollinson & Associates
P.O. Box 7381
Boulder, Colorado 80306
A C G

Elizabeth St. John
Soul Portraits
2325 Spruce   #2
Boulder, Colorado 80302
C

Ellen Steinberg
Metaphysically Speaking
1920 South Locust
Denver, Colorado 80302
C G

Services

Academy of Parapsychology and
   Medicine
P.O. Box 36121
Denver, Colorado 80227
O P S

The Center of Light and Truth
3360 Fourth Street
Boulder, Colorado 80302
C N O

Choices and Connections
Human Potential Resources
P.O. Box 1057

Boulder, Colorado 80306
D

Colorado Headquarters for
The Tibetan Foundation
146 West Fifth Avenue
Denver, Colorado 80204
O

Evergreen Wellness Center
P.O. Box 994
Evergreen, Colorado 80439
N O

Gold Lake
2500 North Broadway
Boulder, Colorado 80302
R

House of Paper Ships
236 Walnut
Fort Colins, Colorado 80524
A B G

ISIS
5701 East Colfax
Denver, Colorado 80220
A B G V

Metaforms
P.O. Box 2262
Boulder, Colorado 80306
   (sculptures that assist in channeling)

NicNacNook Metaphysical Books
4280 Morrison Road
Denver, Colorado 80219
B G S

The Portal
10050 Ralston Road   Suite E
Arvada, Colorado 80004
A B G

School of Metaphysics
1643 Galena

Beulah, Colorado 80010
A B G N O V
   or
133 West Mill Street
Colorado Springs, Colorado
   80903

Spiritual Science Institute
P.O. Box 637
Broomfield, Colorado 80020
A C G O R S

Transcendental Typing
Susan Smith
(303) 477-7348
   (transcripts of channeling sessions)

Truth Center
Seth Conference Committee
4068 South Broadway
Englewood, Colorado 80110
C G O R

Universalian
P.O. Box 6243
Denver, Colorado 80206
C N

Vision Light
6569 South Keim Road
Evergreen, Colorado 80439
A C S

CONNECTICUT

Channelers

Elizabeth Hawkins
139 Broad Street
Middletown, Connecticut 06457
C

Jean Loomis
116 Montowese Street

Branford, Connecticut 06405
A C G

Elizabeth Lynn
P.O. Box 606
Ivoryton, Connecticut 06442
A C G

Pat Rodegast
c/o Val Mylonas
37 Fairfield Place
Fairfield, Connecticut 06430
A C P S V

Services

Academy of Religion and Psychi-
   cal Research
P.O. Box 614
Bloomfield, Connecticut 06002
M O

Aquarian Center
116 Montowese Street
Branford, Connecticut 06405
A G V

The Center for Gnostic Educa-
   tion
P.O. Box 606
Ivoryton, Connecticut 06442
C O S

A Course in Miracles
50 Gungy Road
Lyme, Connecticut 06731
G O

Fenton Valley Press
657 Chaffeeville Road
Storrs, Connecticut 06268
P

Mystic Light Association
P.O. Box 57
West Mystic, Connecticut 06388
C G O S

New Age Exchange
80 Rising Trail Road
Middletown, Connecticut
    06457
N

The Psychic Journal
Charlton Publications
Charlton Building
Derby, Connecticut 06418
M

Pymander
361 Post Road West
Westport, Connecticut 06880
A B

The Tav Center
36 Weston Road
Westport, Connecticut 06880
C G O

Unicorn Books
219A Danbury Road
New Milford, Connecticut
    06776
A B G V

DELAWARE

Channelers

Estrillita
Box 259
Dover, Delaware
C

Services

Chrysalis Center
1008 Miltown Road
Wilmington, Delaware 19808
O

DISTRICT OF COLUMBIA

Services

New Realities
Heldref Publications
4000 Albemarle Street NW
Washington, D.C. 20016
M

The Psychic Observer
Box 8606
Washington, D.C. 20011
N

The Psychic Observer and
    Chimes
5606 16th Street NW
Washington, D.C. 20011
M

Yes! Inc.
1035 31st Street NW
Washington, D.C. 20007
A B V

FLORIDA

Channelers

Jeanette
Cosmic Lightbearers
P.O. Box 4112
Key West, Florida 33041
A C G

Paul Johnson
112 Shadow Lake Drive
Longwood, Florida 32779
A C V

Paul Norris McClain
19610 N.E. 26th Avenue

N. Miami Beach, Florida 33180
C G N

Renate Perelom
P.O. Box 4845
Key West, Florida 33401
A C G

Carolyn Shuck
W. Spring Leaf Lane
Lecanto, Florida 32661
A C

Services

Agartha Secret City
1618 Ponce de Leon
Coral Gables, Florida 33134
A B

Athene
2996 McFarlene Road
Coconut Grove, Florida 31333
B S

Awareness Research Foun-
dation
1518 Lee Street
Polk Street Station
Hollywood, Florida 33020
N O P

The Coordinate Point
P.O. Box 520
Oviedo, Florida 32765
O

Cosmic Book Center
9919 N. Highway
Thonotosassa, Florida 33592
A B

Friendly Contacts Associates
Box 10011
15 Myrtle Drive
Umatilla, Florida 32784

O S

New Age Books
2965 W. State Road   Suite 3000
Longwood, Florida 32779
A B

Parapsychology–Psychic Science
Journal
P.O. Box 60–0927
Miami, Florida 33160
M

The Psychic & Astrological
Cruise Club of North
America
P.O. Box 1184
Venice, Florida 34282
(cruises)

Spiritual Advisory Council
2965 West State Road 434
Suite 300
Longwood, Florida 32779
C O S

WHVH
4154 Herschell Street
Jacksonville, Florida 32110
A B V

GEORGIA

Channelers

Kent & Morgan L. Benedict
982 N. Main Street
Stone Mountain Village, Georgia
30083
C G S

Tim Smith
3120 Maple Drive
Atlanta, Georgia 30066
A C G S V

Services

Alexandrian Temple of Light and
  Institute
235 Berwick Drive
Atlanta, Georgia 30328
M O S

Arthur Ford Academy
P.O. Box 767121
Roswell, Georgia 30076
A C S

Avalon Center
3120 Maple Drive
Atlanta, Georgia 30305
A B G

Patricia Hayes School of Inner
  Development
P.O. Box 767121
Roswell, Georgia 30076
O S

Psychic Connections
P.O. Box 670022
Marietta, Georgia 30066
N O

Rainbow Earth
982 N. Main Street
Stone Mountain Village, Georgia
  30083
P S

Sphinx Learning Center
1510 Piedmont Avenue
Atlanta, Georgia 30324
A B G

Upward Search
4620 Wiecua Road   #39
Atlanta, Georgia 30342
N

HAWAII

Channelers

Alice Ann Parker
59-075 Puula Road
Haleiwa, Hawaii 96712
A C G N S

Services

Common Ground
47-155 Okana Road
Kaneohe, Hawaii 69744
N

The Illumined Way
Clearlight Associates
4265 Round Top Drive
Honolulu, Hawaii 96822
C G S

IDAHO

Channelers

Vern Overlee
19 Scott Street
Post Falls, Idaho 83854
C P

Services

The Farm
P.O. Box 579
Sagle, Idaho 83860
G O R S

School of Metaphysics
219 North Third Street
Belleville, Idaho 62220
A B G N O V

ILLINOIS

Channelers

Shelley Amdur
4723 N. Sacramento
Chicago, Illinois 60656
C

Ruth Berger
7925 N. Lincoln Avenue
Skokie, Illinois 60077
C G N O

Branda Carl
4800 South Lake Park
Suite #707
Chicago, Illinois 60615
A C G

Marcella Daniels
P.O. Box 1946
Rockford, Illinois 61110
A C

Robert Dubiel
1329 W. Touhy
Chicago, Illinois 60626
A C G

Jim and Judy Flanigan
4031 Main Street
Downers Grove, Illinois 60515
C

Marie Johnson
6047 Talman
Chicago, Illinois 60629
A C

Maxine Jones
818 Washington
Evanston, Illinois 60202
A C G V

Jill Lockhart
Apt. 9S   180 Lake Drive

Clarendon Hills, Illinois 60514
C

A. Frank Miller
1222 Laurel Lane
Schaumburg, Illinois 60172
C

Pat Shenberg
4870 West Route 6
Morris, Illinois 60450
C

Services

Central PSI Research Institute
c/o Ms. Terry Brennan
125075 Robert Drive
Naperville, Illinois 60565
N O

Crystal Light Centre
P.O. Box 1946
Rockford, Illinois 61110
A G N V

Fate
500 Hyacinth Place
Highland Park, Illinois 60035
M

The Greater Chicagoland Psychic
   Directory
P.O. Box 205
Oaklawn, Illinois 60454
D

Intuitive Explorations
Box 561
Quincy, Illinois 62306
N

The Monthly Aspectarian
P.O. Box 1342
Morton Grove, Illinois 60053
N

New Age Resource Directory
P.O. Box 1491
Elk Grove Village, Illinois
   60009
D

The Resource Center
3434 Central
Evanston, Illinois 60201
A B V

Sunrise
P.O. Box 113
Warrenville, Illinois 60035
N

U.S. Psychotronics Association
3459 W. Montrose
Chicago, Illinois 60618
A N S V

INDIANA

Channelers

Marguerite Carter
Box 807   Dept. 707
Indianapolis, Indiana 46206
A C

Marghee
67-27 Kennedy Avenue
Hammond, Indiana 46323
A C

Services

Keller's Metaphysical Book Center
9431 West County Line Road
Camby, Indiana 46113
A B V

IOWA

Services

Hiawatha Book Company
7567 NE 102 Avenue
Bondurant, Iowa 50035
B

School of Metaphysics
1421 26th Street
Des Moines, Iowa 50310
A B G N O

KANSAS

Channelers

Marion Brenner
Certified Channel
The Tibetan Foundation
609 Anita Drive
Haysville, Kansas 67060
A C G

Carol Ann Gragg
Certified Channel
The Tibetan Foundation
532 South Terrace
Wichita, Kansas 67218
A C G

Services

Dharmasala
9515 Provincial Lane
Wichita, Kansas 67212
G R S

Journey Books
2717 East Central
Wichita, Kansas 67214
A B G

Pathways
Box 534
Derby, Kansas 67037
N O

School of Metaphysics
1108 N. 26th Street
Kansas City, Kansas 66102
B G O

Self-Actualization and Enlightenment Center
2717 E. Central
Wichita, Kansas 67214
O S

KENTUCKY

Channelers

Denver Campbell, Jr.
10 Kyles Lanes   #2
Fort Thomas, Kentucky 41075
C G

Services

L/L Research
P.O. Box 5195
Louisville, Kentucky 40205
A N P

LOUISIANA

Channelers

Katherine Krefft, Ph.D.
Transpersonal Psychologist
2245 College Drive   Suite #80
Baton Rouge, Louisiana 70808
A C G S

Services

Fountain of Light
7877 Jefferson Highway
Baton Rouge, Louisiana 70809
A B G N V

The Louisiana Society for Psych-
ical Research
Nell Smith, Director
39376 Highway 929
Prairieville, Louisiana 70769
N O S

School of Metaphysics
448 Wiltz
Baton Rouge, Louisiana 70806
A B G N O

MAINE

Channelers

Brother Abaddon
Box 201
Cape Cottage, Maine 04107
A C

Pat Balzer
Certified Channeler
The Tibetan Foundation
P.O. Box 126
Richmond, Maine 04357
C G

Mary E. Carriero
P.O. Box 387
Kittery, Maine 03904
C P

Services

Brotherhood
Gentle Wind Retreat

P.O. Box 387
Kittery, Maine 03904
R

The Society of Mary Magdalen
Box 201
Cape Cottage, Maine 04107
O

MARYLAND

Channelers

Sarah Estep
726 Dill Road
Severna Park, Maryland 21146
C

Elisabeth Y. Fitzhugh
Box 5429
Takoma Park, Maryland
C

Services

Inner Dimension Cruises
26 W. Susquehanna Avenue
Baltimore, Maryland 21204
S

LIGHT
P.O. Box 644
Silver Spring, Maryland 20901
O

MASSACHUSETTS

Channelers

Elwood Babbitt
c/o General Delivery
Northfield, Massachusetts 01360
A C G P S

Crow Speaks
c/o Box 57
Wendell Depot, Massachusetts
  01380
C N

Marion McIntire
277 Main Street
Northhampton, Massachusetts
  01060
C

Mary Frances Platt, M.Ed.
16 Center Street   Suite 308
Northampton, Massachusetts
  01060
C

Laurie Sieser
Shelburne Center Road
Shelburne, Massachusetts 01370
C V

Services

ABYSS
34 Cottage Street
Easthampton, Massachusetts
  01027
A B

Bergin & Garvey
670 Amherst Road
South Hadley, Massachusetts
  01705
P

Beyond Words
150 Main Street
Northampton, Massachusetts
  01060
A B G V

The Center of the Light
P.O. Box 540

Great Barrington, Massachusetts
   01230
O R S

East West Journal
17 Station Street
Brookline, Massachusetts 02146
M

ECWM
P.O. Box 2508
Framingham Center, Massachu-
   setts 01701
O

Genesis
Spiritual Life Center
53 Mill Street
Westfield, Massachusetts 01085
C G S

Interface
522 Main Street
Watertown, Massachusetts
G S

Macromedia
Jeff Volk
P.O. Box 1223
Brookline, Massachusetts 02146
G MP S V

Many Hands
Thorne's Market
Main Street
Northampton, Massachusetts
   01060
D M

New Age Journal
342 Western Avenue
Brighton, Massachusetts 02135
M N

New England Sound Healers,
   Inc.

Jonathan S. Goldman
42 Baker Avenue
Lexington, Massachusetts 02173
A G N S

New Pathways
103 Goldencrest Avenue
Waltham Masachusetts 02154
B

New Visions
10 Taconic Street
Pittsfield, Massachusetts 01201
N

Pyramid
214 Derby Street
Salem, Massachusetts
B G

Sophia
16 Main Street
Amherst, Massachusetts 01085
A B

The Spirit's Voice
P.O. Box 158
Newton, Massachusetts 02161
N

The Synthesis Center
178A North Pleasant
Amherst, Massachusetts 01002
S

The Univercolian
Box 292
Dalton, Massachusetts 01226
N O

MICHIGAN

Channelers

Marcia Becker Emery, Ph.D
Psychotherapist

3512 McCoy SE
Grand Rapids, Michigan 49506
A C G

Cathy Jones
Certified Channel
The Tibetan Foundation
432 Buckingham
Flint, Michigan 48507
C

Rainbow Bridge Group
23415 Ann Arbor Trail
Dearborn Heights, Michigan
    48127
C G

Services

Crazy Wisdom
206 North Fourth Avenue
Ann Arbor, Michigan 48104
A B C G V

Michigan Metaphysical Society
3018 12 Mile Road
Berkley, Michigan 48072
A B G O

Middle Earth
2791 East 14 Mile Road
Sterling Heights, Michigan 48077
B

The Mountain Books
302 South Waverly
Lansing, Michigan 48072
B G S

Mystic Healing Center
P.O. Box 565
Grand Haven, Michigan 49417
C G O

Phenomenews
2821 North Woodward

Royal Oak, Michigan 48072
M

The Store for the Miracle
    Minded
11200 East 11 Mile Road
Warren, Michigan 48089
A B V

Zetetic Scholar
Department of Sociology
Eastern Michigan University
Ypsilanti, Michigan 48197
M

MINNESOTA

Channelers

Paul Michael Davies
3105 Girard Avenue South
Minneapolis, Minnesota 55408
A C G N S V

Sheila Moran
2400 Lyndale South   #2A
Minneapolis, Minnesota 55405
C G

Services

Evenstar
2035 Riverside Avenue
Minneapolis, Minnesota 55454
A B G

Personal Growth Network
6490 Excelsior Blvd.
Minneapolis, Minnesota 55426
D

Sunsight
612 W. Lake Street
Minneapolis, Minnesota 55408
A B C G N V

Wings of Light
Quest Enterprises
464 Second Street   Suite B
Excelsior, Minnesota 55331
M

MISSISSIPPI

Services

School of Metaphysics
4526 Hanging Moss Road
Jackson, Mississippi 39206
B G N O

MISSOURI

Channelers

Barry and Angela Spath
P.O. Box 2270
Florissant, Missouri
63032
A C G V

Services

Alchemist Shop
2521 Woodson Road
Overland, Missouri 63114
B G

Astrology, Mysticism & the Oc-
    cult
P.O. Box 1832
Kansas City, Missouri 64141
M

Directory of the Occult and Para-
    normal
P.O. Box 1832
Kansas City, Missouri 64141
D

Doorways to the Mind
Mind Development Association
Box 29396
Sappington, Missouri 63126
M O

The Magick Lantern
1715 Westport Road
Kansas City, Missouri 64111
A B

New Life Research
Box 22467
Kansas City, Missouri 64113
A

School of Metaphysics Head-
    quarters
Box 15
Windyville, Missouri 65783
    or
210 Third Avenue
Clayton, Missouri 65201
A B C G S V

Spiritual Development Services
P.O. Box 2279
Florissant, Missouri 63032
C G O

MONTANA

Channelers

Bernie Long
1281 Grubstake Center
Billings, Montana 59105
C G

Melva M. Miluck
1215 W. Durston   #119
Bozeman, Montana 59715
G S

Elizabeth Clare Prophet
Box A
Livingston, Montana 59047
A C G P R S V

Services

Holistic Life Seminars
P.O. Box 1682
Helena, Montana 59624
S

Mind Development & Control
    Association
P.O. Box 29396
Sappington, Montana 63126
O P

NEBRASKA

Channelers

The Silver Circle
1265 South Cotner
    No. 19
Lincoln, Nebraska 68510
A B G V

Spectra
P.O. Box 241013
Omaha, Nebraska 68214
N O

NEVADA

Channelers

Jason Winters
4055 Spencer Street
    Suite 235
Las Vegas, Nevada 89101
C

Services

Books Plus
1020 South Wells Avenue
Reno, Nevada 89502
A B G

Joy Lake Mountain Seminar
Att: Alan Morvay
P.O. Box 1328
Reno, Nevada 89504
G R S

NEW HAMPSHIRE

Channelers

Myrna Malone
Brian Smith
P.O. Box 622
Fitzwilliam, New Hampshire
    03447
C P

Eleanor Moore
210 Old Jaffrey Road
Peterborough, New Hampshire
    03458
A C

Meredith Lady Young
c/o Stillpoint
P.O. Box 640
Meetinghouse Road
Walpole, New Hampshire 03608
C P S

Services

Earth Star Journal
P.O. Box 110
Temple, New Hampshire 03084
M

Stillpoint Publishing
P.O. Box 640
Walpole, New Hampshire 03608
A N P

NEW JERSEY

Channelers

Cher Carden
P.O. Box 1301
Princeton, New Jersey 08540
A C G S

Holly Lynn
Box 1037
Ocean Gate, New Jersey 08740
C G

Colleen Schumacher
149 Warren Avenue
Fort Lee, New Jersey 07024
C

Services

Course in Miracles
Miracle Manor
P.O. Box 1036
New Brunswick, New Jersey
  08903
G O R S

Free Spirit
160 Main Street
Flemington, New Jersey 08822
A B

Inner Light
Box 753
New Brunswick, New Jersey
  08903
O

Psychic Guide/Psychic Fair
Network News
215 Little Falls Road
Fairfield, New Jersey 07006
N

NEW MEXICO

Channelers

Alexandria
Psychic Associates
103 Catron Street   No. 18
Santa Fe, New Mexico 87501
C G

Vicki V. Baer
P.O. Box 1339
Los Alamos, New Mexico 87544
A C G

Page Bryant
P.O. Box 4384
Albuquerque, New Mexico 87196
A C G

Rick Light
Certified Channel
The Tibetan Foundation
2571 36th Street
Los Alamos, New Mexico 87544
C G

Alex Lucker
103 Catron Street
Santa Fe, New Mexico 87501
A C G S

David Paladin
Box 11942
Albuquerque, New Mexico 87192
A C

Jamie Sams

535 Cordova Road   Suite #430
Santa Fe, New Mexico 87501
A C S

Salli Lou West
546 Onate Place
Santa Fe, New Mexico 87501
A C G

Services

The Ark
133 Romero Street
Santa Fe, New Mexico 87501
B

Brotherhood of Life
110 Dartmouth SE
Albuquerque, New Mexico 87106
B

Interdimensional Temple of
   Light/ Crystal Connection
   Newsletter
P.O. Box 1339
Los Alamos, New Mexico 87544
N O P

Metaphysical Motivation Institute
641 Soudderth Drive
Ruidoso, New Mexico 88345
A B G V

Sun
P.O. Box 4384
Albuquerque, New Mexico 87196
A P

Sun Publishing Company
P.O. Box 5588
Santa Fe, New Mexico 87502
P

NEW YORK

Channelers

Audrey Arbe
412 8th Avenue
New York, New York 10011
C

Nancy Azara
46 Great Jones Street
New York, New York 10009
C

Dee Betts
11 First Street
Lily Dale, New York 14752
C

Beth Botley
Certified Channel
The Tibetan Foundation
110 West 96th Street   Apt. 5A
New York, New York 10025
C G

Lauren Chambers
316 East 11th Street
New York, New York 10003
A C

Lauren Theodore Dascher
230 Riverside Drive
New York, New York 10025
A C G

Devorah Devi
702 West End Avenue   Apt. 3B
New York, New York 10025
A C G S

Leisha Douglas
Psychotherapist
RD #2   Box 195
Amawalk Road

208

CHANNELERS

Katonah, New York 10536
A C

Andrea Dynan
807 East 18th Street
Brooklyn, New York 11230
C

Richard B. Forschmidt
30 Lotus Lane
Westbury, New York 11590
C

Rev. Ojela Frank
P.O. Box 327
New City, New York 10956
A C G

Steven and Donna Hirsch
86 Whispering Hills Drive
Chester, New York 10918
A C

Alan Kardec
P.O. Box 6571
Syracuse, New York 13217
C

Laurie Lamb
135 Ocean Parkway
Brooklyn, New York 11218
C

Ann Levinson
20 Fifth Avenue
New York, New York 10011
C G S

Daniel Logan
Box 12
West Hurley, New York 12491
A C

Timothy J. Long
250 Mulberry Street   Apt. #3
New York, New York 10012
C G

Debra Lynch
75 Bank Street
New York, New York 10014
A C N S V

Margaret Macauley
7 Kings Highway
Warwick, New York 10990
A C G

Elizabeth Mass, M.A.
P.O. Box 1010
Staten Island, New York 10314
A C G S

Michael Morgan
230 West 76th Street   Apt. #2
New York, New York 10023
A C N V

Alexander Murray
172 West 79th Street   Apt. 18C
New York, New York 10024
A C G S

R. Randall
Through Grace
234 East 58th Street   Apt. #22
New York, New York 10022
A C G

Cynthia Richter
635 East 9th Street   Apt. #1
New York, New York 10009
A C G S

J'aime Schelz
204 Hamilton Avenue
New Rochelle, New York 10801
A C G P S

Rose Shatzel
2 Third Street
Lily Dale, New York 14752
C

Shirley Colkins Smith
14 Cottage Row
Lily Dale, New York 14752
A C G

Mark Victor Venaglia
17 West 24th Street
New York, New York 10011
A C G S

Susan Watkins
Box 217
Dundee, New York 14837
C

John C. White
P.O. Box 1166
Lily Dale, New York 14752
A C G

Mark Zweigler
Box 1836
Cathedral Station
New York, New York 10025
C

Services

ABNOSTICORUAF
86 Whispering Hills Drive
Chester, New York
A C D

American Society for Psychical
    Research
Five West 73rd Street
New York, New York 10023
M N O S

Beyond Reality
30 Amarillo Drive
Nanuet, New York 10954
M

Central Premonitions Registry
P.O. Box 482
Times Square Station
New York, New York 10023
O

Conscious Connection
50 West 77th Street
New York, New York 10024
O

Cosmic Contact
Channeling Referral Service
Att: Mike Goodrich
26 East 13th Street
New York, New York 10003
O

East/West
78 Fifth Avenue
New York, New York 10011
A B G S

Foundation for a Course in Mira-
    cles
P.O. Box 783
Crompond, New York 10517
A C N O V

Free Spirit
137 6th Avenue
Brooklyn, New York 11217
M

Holistic Health Works
P.O. Box 327
New City, New York 10956
A C G N P V

I.N.D.I.A.
(Inter-National Development,
Improvement & Assistance)
315 Fifth Avenue
New York, New York 10016
C G S

Integrity Electronics & Research
Lynn A. Surgalla
558 Breckenridge Street
Buffalo, New York 14222
G P S

Kendall Enterprises
Seth Video
P.O. Box 5258
Rockefeller Center
New York, New York 10185
MP V

Miracle
109 Utica
Ithaca, New York 14850
C G

The Mustard Seed
High Rock Graphics
38 Sunrise Avenue
Katonah, New York 10536

Parapsychology Foundation
228 East 71st Street
New York, New York 10021
N O

Parapsychology Institute of
   America
Dr. Stephen Kaplan and Max
   Toth, Directors
P.O. Box 252
Elmhurst, New York 11373
N O

Phoenicia Pathwork Center
Box 66
Phoenicia, New York 12464
G O S

Raj Talks
Riverrun Press
P.O. Box 367
Piermont Avenue

Piermont, New York 10968
A G M N

Spiritual Frontiers
390 West End Avenue   Apt. 9A
New York, New York 10024
N O S

Samuel Weiser
132 East 24th Street
New York, New York 10010
A B

Whole Life
89 Fifth Avenue   Suite 600
New York, New York 10003
M

NORTH CAROLINA

Channelers

Richard Mansbach
Certified Channeler
The Tibetan Foundation
1705 Audubon Road
Chapel Hill, North Carolina
   27514
C G

Sandra Price-Haberer
P.O. Box 337
Clyde, North Carolina 28721
A C

Reverend Micki Rouse
P.O. Box 752
Menbane, North Carolina 27302
C

Services

The Awareness Research Foundation

Helen I. Hoag, Executive Director
DeSoto Square No. 29
35 Ritter Road
Hayesville, North Carolina
A N O

Happiness Now
5303 West Market Street
Greensboro, North Carolina
  27419
A B G V

Metascience Foundation
P.O. Box 737
Franklin, North Carolina 28734
O

New Age Tape and Book Club
105 WNC Mall
Black Mountain, North Carolina
  28711
A B

Path of Light
3427 Denson Place
Charlotte, North Carolina 28215
D

Psychic Dimensions/Psychic
  Foundation of Knowledge, Inc.
P.O. Box 25504
Charlotte, North Carolina 28229
N O

Psychical Research Foundation
P.O. Box 3356
Chapel Hill, North Carolina
  27514
O P

The Sun
412 West Rosemary Street
Chapel Hill, North Carolina
  27514
N O

Theta: The Journal of the Psychical Research Foundation
W. G. Roll, Editor
Duke Station
Durham, North Carolina 27706
M

OHIO

Channelers

David Johns
4129 Rabbit Run Drive
Cleveland, Ohio 44144
C G

Allen LePar
P.O. Box 2276
North Canton, Ohio 44720
A C P

Coyote Pohatan
3877 West 162 Street
Cleveland, Ohio 44111
A C G S

Services

Books of Light
4082 Clotts Road
P.O. Box 30975
Columbus, Ohio 43230
P

Manifestations
31 Colonial Arcade
Cleveland, Ohio 44115
A B V

Occult Book Shoppe
1849 West 65th Street
Cleveland, Ohio 44102
A B V

Psychic Science International
7514 Belleplain Drive
Dayton, Ohio 45424
N O P

SOLAR
P.O. Box 2276
North Canton, Ohio 44720
N

OKLAHOMA

Channelers

Amelia
P.O. Box 6582
Moore, Oklahoma 73153
A C G S

Daze
5147 South Harvard   Suite 288
Tulsa, Oklahoma 74137
A C G S

Krysnal
1924 Beverly Hills
Norman, Oklahoma 73069
A C G S

Carol Parish
P.O. Box 1274
Tahlequah, Oklahoma 74464
C G

Services

Aquarius Rising
Promotor of Psychic Fairs/
   Psychic Talent Agency
P.O. Box 691439
Tulsa, Oklahoma 74169
G N S V

The Organization of Psychic Research Associates

Box 30416
Midwest City, Oklahoma 73140
C N O

School of Metaphysics
1419 South Quincy
Tulsa, Oklahoma 74120
A B G N O V

Sparrow Hawk Village
P.O. Box 1274
Tahlequah, Oklahoma 77464
C G O

OREGON

Channelers

Rev. Jackie Ramirez
P.O. Box 13
Lebanon, Oregon 97355
A C G

Services

Anchor of Golden Light
P.O. Box 451
Grants Pass, Oregon 97526
N O

Cosmic Voyage
P.O. Box 1116B
McMinnville, Oregon 97128
N

The Golden Mean
1253 Siskiyou Boulevard
Ashland, Oregon 97520
A B G V

Perelandra
790 East 11th Avenue
Eugene, Oregon 97401
A B

PENNSYLVANIA

Channelers

Michael Diamond
28 South Strawberry Street
Philadelphia, Pennsylvania 19106
A C G S

Phyllis Givens
127 South Main Street
New Hope, Pennsylvania 18938
A C P

Karen Lander Hughes
502 Emily Circle
West Chester, Pennsylvania
  19382
C

John & Chase Pawlik
2900 Glenwood Road
Camp Hill, Pennsylvania 17011
C G S P

Ann Peckman
969 Valleyvista Avenue
Pittsburgh, Pennsylvania 18707
C O R S

Sheila Reynolds
P.O. Box 155
Washington Crossing, Pennsylvania 18977
C

Samuel Speaks
P.O. Box 66
Springhouse, Pennsylvania 19477
C

Services

The Channeling Center
7400 Fourth Avenue

Melrose Park, Pennsylvania
  19047
C G N O

Creative Energy Options
909 Sunnytown Pike
Springhouse, Pennsylvania 19477
C G

Hemetro
127 S. Main
New Hope, Pennsylvania 18938
A B S V

Life Nourishment Center
Norman Mitchell, Director
712 Trenton Road
Longhorne, Pennsylvania 17108
A M N O S

Life Spectrums/Rainbow
P.O. Box 373
Harrisburg, Pennsylvania 19477
A G N O S

A New Age Center
502 Emily Circle
West Chester, Pennsylvania
  19382
C O

New Frontiers
129 North 13th Street
Philadelphia, Pennsylvania 19107
M

Sign of Aquarius
815 Copeland Street
Pittsburgh, Pennsylvania 15232
B

Spiritual Frontiers/Northeast Retreat
Elizabethtown College
Elizabeth, Pennsylvania 18707
C O R S

Spiritual Science Institute of
  Philadelphia
2650 Meetinghouse Road
Jamison, Pennsylvania 18929
O

Unicorn
8 West Main Street
Hummelstown, Pennsylvania
  17036
A B

RHODE ISLAND

Services

Body, Mind & Spirit
Box 701
Providence, Rhode Island 02901
M

Metascience Foundation
Box 32
Kingston, Rhode Island 02881
M O

The New Age Metaphysical
  Bookstore
30 Canal Street
Westerly, Rhode Island 02891
A B G S V

TENNESSEE

Channelers

Barbara Carlon
1717 W. Adair Drive
Knoxville, Tennessee 37918
A C G

Services

The Out-of-Book Experience
2809 West End Avenue
Nashville, Tennessee 37203
B

TEXAS

Channelers

Rev. Pamelle Coleman
302 East Ferguson
Pharr, Texas 78571
A C G

Harriette Hartly
2006 Winewood
Arlington, Texas 76013
A C

D. Jones
8326 Windwillow Drive
Houston, Texas 77040
C

Services

Aquarian Age
5603 Chaucer
Houston, Texas 77098
A B

Austin Seth Center
Box 7786
Austin, Texas 78713
O S

Centric
Esoteric Philosophy Center
523 Lovett Boulevard
Houston, Texas 77006
M O

F.L.A.M.E.
Meta-Scoop
1004 Live Oak
Arlington, Texas 76012
M N O

Mind Science Foundation
8301 Broadway   Suite 100
San Antonio, Texas 78209
N O S

National Psychic Directory
P.O. Box 476300
Garland, Texas 75047
D

The Quantis Report
P.O. Box 2730
Austin, Texas 78755
N

Reality Change
P.O. Box 7786
Austin, Texas 78713
M

San Antonio Quest
725 W. Ashby
San Antonio, Texas 78212
A B S V

UTAH

Services

Kosmon Voice
Box 664
Salt Lake City, Utah 84110
N

VERMONT

Channelers

Barbara Bartley
Box 434
Hartland, Vermont 05048
C N

Judith Hope Davis
Life & Light Center
Bull Run Road
Northfield, Vermont 05663
A C G

Mary Peck
RR 1
Box 1335
Johnson, Vermont 05656
A C G V

Services

Clear Light at Klara Simpla
10 Main Street
Wilmington, Vermont 05363
C G S

The Psychic
Mora Press
P.O. Box 130
Canaan, Vermont 05903
P

Rainbow Connections
P.O. Box 264
Wilmington, Vermont 05363
P

VIRGINIA

Channelers

Daniel Clay
Box 100

Troutdale, Virginia 24378
C

Tam Mossman
P.O. Box 3295
Charlottesville, Virginia 22903
A C

John Oliver
SRI
Box 29
Earlysville, Virginia 22936
A C G N S

Eileen Rota
829 Lynhaven Pkwy
Suite 114–215
Virginia Beach, Virginia 23452
C G

Services

Association for Research and En-
    lightenment
P.O. Box 595
Virginia Beach, Virginia 23451
M N O P S
(Edgar Cayce Materials)

Heritage
P.O. Box 71
319 Laskin Road
Virginia Beach, Virginia 23458
A B G

Heritage Store
P.O. Box 444
Virginia Beach, Virginia 23458
D P
(specializing exclusively in Edgar
    Cayce Materials)

Metapsychology: The Journal of
    Discarnate Intelligence
P.O. Box 3295

Charlottesville, Virginia 22903
M

Open Channels
829 Lunhaven Parkway
Suite 114–215
Virginia Beach, Virginia 23452
C O

Parapsychological Association
P.O. Box 7503
Alexandria, Virginia 22307
O P

PSI News
P.O. Box 7503
Alexandria, Virginia 22307
N O

Seven Oaks Pathwork Center
Route 1
Box 86
Madison, Virginia 22727
R

Synchronicity
M.S.H. Foundation
Route 1
Box 192–B
Faber, Virginia 22938
A C G S

WASHINGTON

Channelers

Michelle Bernards
Point Hudson
Port Townsend, Washington
    98368
C G P

Count Carnette
1632 Broadway

Seattle, Washington 98122
C

Teresa Carol
1912 E. 72nd Street
Tacoma, Washington 98404
C

MariJo Donais
2221 E. 30th Street
Vancouver, Washington 98663
A C G

Barbara Easton
1015 S. 30th Court
Renton, Washington 98055
C G

J.Z. Knight
P.O. Box 1210
Yelm, Washington 98597
A C G P S B V

Robert Ranjel
226 S. 312 Street
Federal Way, Washington 98003
C

Gail Richardson
11709 Pawnee Drive S.W.
Tacoma, Washington 98499
C G

Ruth Soderstrom
1912 E. 72nd Street
Tacoma, Washington 98404
A C

Shirley Teabo
226 S. 312th Street
Federal Way, Washington 98003
C

Pault Tuttle
Kairos, Inc.
P.O. Box 71280

Seattle, Washington 98107
A C

Services

Akasha Metaphysics
1124 State Street
Bellingham, Washington 98225
A B G

The Book Nook
722 Summitview
Yakima, Washington 98902
B

Conversations with Raj
Kairos, Inc
P.O. Box 71280
Seattle, Washington 98107
N

The Flying Unicorn
19740 G 7th Avenue
P.O. Box 1960
Poulsbo, Washington 98370
A B G

Insight Northwest
Box 95341
Seattle, Washington 98145
M

Metaphysical Research Society
4023 North Wall
Spokane, Washington 99205
N O

The Open Door
West 1011 Sprague Avenue
Spokane, Washington 99204
A B G S

Phoenix
9312 NE 76th Street
Vancouver, Washington 98662
B

Phoenix Rising
118 Taylor Street
Port Townsend, Washington
  98368
A B C G S

Psychic Energy Center
1912 E. 72nd Street
Tacoma, Washington 98404
C O

Ramtha Dialogue
Church I AM
P.O. Box 1210
Yelm, Washington 98597
A C G P R S V

Revelations of Awareness
Box 115
Olympia, Washington 98507
N

Sixth Sense
226 S. 312th Street
Federal Way, Washington 98003
C O

WEST VIRGINIA

Channelers

Lilly Fluger
Box 157
Fayetteville, West Virginia 25840
A C

Services

The Direct Mind Experience
1686 Marshall Street
Benwood, West Virginia 26031
N O

TAT Journal
1686 Marshall Street
Benwood, West Virginia 26031
N O

WISCONSIN

Channelers

Hilda First
Route 1
Chaseburg, Wisconsin 54621
C P

Services

Circle Network News
Box 9013
Madison, Wisconsin 53202
M

Coming Changes
937 St. Mary's Street
De Pere, Wisconsin 54115
N

House of Scorpio
5924 W. Burnham
Milwaukee, Wisconsin 53219
B G

New Frontiers Center
RR 1
Oregon, Wisconsin 53575
G N O

Sanctum Regnum
615 N. Milwaukee Street
Milwaukee, Wisconsin 53202
B

CANADA

Channelers

Joseph Cohen
P.O. Box 7228A
Toronto, Ontario
M5W 1X8, Canada
A C G S

Helmut Hoehl
P.O. Box 551
Edmonton, Alberta
T6C 4E9, Canada
C G

Mary Kenny
1363 West 15th Street
North Vancouver, British Colum-
   bia
V7P 1N1, Canada
C

Cliff Preston
P.O. Box 35
Orangeville, Ontario
L9W 225, Canada
A C G

Services

Common Ground
Box 34090   Station D
Vancouver, British Columbia
V6J 4MI, Canada
M

Crystal Journey
P.O. Box 7228A
Toronto, Ontario
M5W 1X8, Canada
N

Inner Life
Toronto Aquarian
214 Glengarry Avenue
Toronto, Ontario
M5M 1E4, Canada
N

Other Dimensions
Box 2269
Salmon Arm, British Columbia
VOE 2TO, Canada
A B O R S

Pine Ridge Center
P.O. Box 362
Pickering, Ontario
L1V 2R6, Canada
C G S

The Psychic & Astrological
   Cruise
P.O. Box 1957
Station A
London, Ontario
N6A 5J4, Canada
S
(cruises)

Spiritual Science Fellowship
1974 de Maisonneuve West
Montreal, Quebec
H3H 1K5, Canada
O S

Notes

Introduction: Why Now?

1. Pat Rodegast and Judith Stanton, *Emmanuel's Book*. Weston, Connecticut: Friend's Press, 1985, p. 74.

2. Christian Garcia, "And Now, the 35,000-Year-Old Man." *Time*, December 15, 1986, p. 36.

3. "Voices from Beyond: The Channelers." *People*, January 26, 1987, p. 32.

4. James Cornell, "Psychology and the Millennium." *Psychology Today*, March 1984, p. 34.

5. Ramtha, with Douglas J. Mahr, *Voyage to the New World*. New York: Ballantine Books, 1985, p. 24.

6. *Emmanuel's Book*, p. 215.

7. Charles H. Hapgood, *Voices of Spirit through the Psychic Experience of Elwood Babbit*. New York: Delacorte Press, 1975, p. 250

8. Anthony Brandt, "Ethics: Looking for an Answer." *Esquire*, January 1984, p. 18

9. James Cornell, "Science vs. the Paranormal." *Psychology Today*, March 1984, p. 30.

10. Sheila Ostrander and Lynn Schroeder, *Handbook of PSI Discoveries*. New York: Berkley Books, 1974, p. 278.

11. "Voices from Beyond." *People*, January 26, 1987, p. 30.

12. Art Levine and Cynthia Kyle, "Mystics on Main Street." *U.S. News & World Report*, February 9, 1987, pp. 67–68.

13. "And Now, the 35,000-Year-Old Man," p. 36.

14. "Mystics on Main Street," p. 68.

One: Prophets, Mediums and Mystics

1. Arthur Conan Doyle, *The History of Spiritualism*. New York: Arno Press, 1975, p. 18.
2. *Ibid.*
3. *Ibid.*, p. 54.
4. *Ibid.*, p. 195.
5. Hugh Lynn Cayce, *Venture Inward*. New York: Harper & Row, 1964, pp. 12–13.
6. *Ibid.*, pp. 52–53.
7. *Ibid.*, p. 69.
8. *Ibid.*, p. 72.
9. *Ibid.*, pp. 40–41.
10. Jane Roberts, *Psychic Politics*. New Jersey: Prentice-Hall, 1976, p. 36.
11. Jane Roberts, *The "Unknown" Reality*. New Jersey: Prentice-Hall, 1977, pp. 15–16.
12. *Psychic Politics*, p. 23.
13. Joe Fisher, *The Case for Reincarnation*. Ontario, Canada: William Collins and Sons, 1984, p. 86.
14. Jane Roberts, *The God of Jane*. New Jersey: Prentice-Hall, 1981, p. 4.
15. *Psychic Politics*, pp. 194–95.
16. *Ibid.*, p. 166.
17. Bonnie Silverstein, "Cézanne through a Psychic." *American Artist*, April 1983, pp. 79–81.
18. Jane Roberts, *Adventures in Consciousness*. New Jersey: Prentice-Hall, 1975, p. 35.
19. *The God of Jane*, pp. 39–40.

Two: The Channelers and Their Entities

1. "Voices from Beyond: The Channelers." *People*, January 26, 1987, p. 30.
2. Robert Lindsey, "Teachings of 'Ramtha' Pull Hundreds West." *New York Times*, November 16, 1986, pp. 1, 10.
3. Charles H. Hapgood, *Voices of Spirit through the Psychic Experience of Elwood Babbitt*. New York: Delacorte Press, 1975, p. 279.

4. *Ibid.*, p. 83.

5. *Ibid.*, pp. 285–86.

6. Pat Rodegast and Judith Stanton, *Emmanuel's Book*. Weston, Connecticut: Friend's Press, 1985, p. 117.

7. *Ibid.*, p. 91.

8. Sanaya Roman and Duane Packer, "The Path to Enlightenment." *Birth into Light*, Vol. 2, No. 1, p. 4.

9. Sanaya Roman and Duane Packer, *Opening to Channel: How to Connect with Your Guide*. Tiburon, California: H. J. Kramer, 1987, p. 129.

10. *Birth into Light*, p. 2.

11. *Opening to Channel*, p. 171.

12. Ruth Montgomery and Joanne Garland, *Herald of the New Age*. New York: Fawcett Crest, 1986, p. 231.

13. *Ibid.*, p. 3.

14. *Ibid.*, p. 92.

15. *Ibid.*, p. 99.

16. *Ibid.*, p. 106.

17. *Ibid.*, p. 131.

18. *Ibid.*, p. 149.

19. *Ibid.*

20. *Ibid.*, p. 248.

Bibliography

Bartlett, Helen, "Spirits of New York." *New York Beat*, January 1984, p. 1.

Bowles, Norma, and Fran Hynds, *PSI Search: The Comprehensive Guide to Psychic Phenomena.* New York: Harper & Row, 1978.

Brandt, Anthony, "Ethics: Looking for an Answer." *Esquire*, January 1984, pp. 18, 20.

Cayce, Hugh Lynn, *Venture Inward.* New York: Harper & Row, 1964.

Cronell, James, "Psychology and the Millennium." *Psychology Today*, March 1984, p. 34.

————, "Science vs. the Paranormal." *Psychology Today*, March 1984, pp. 29–30, 34.

Doyle, Arthur Conan, *The History of Spiritualism.* New York: Arno Press, 1975.

Fisher, Joe, *The Case for Reincarnation.* New York: Bantam Books, 1985.

Garcia, Christina, "And Now, the 35,000-Year-Old Man." *Time*, December 15, 1986, p. 36.

Gardner, Martin, "Isness Is Her Business." *New York Review of Books*, pp. 16–18.

Glass, Justine, *They Foresaw the Future.* New York: G. P. Putnam's Sons, 1975.

Hackett, Georgia, and Pamela Abramson, "Ramtha, a Voice from Beyond," *Newsweek*, December 15, 1986, p. 42.

Hapgood, Charles H., *Voices of Spirit through the Psychic Experience of Elwood Babbitt.* New York: Delacorte Press, 1975.

Levine, Art, and Christine Kyle, "Mystics on Main Street." *U.S. News & World Report*, February 9, 1987, pp. 67–69.

Lindsey, Robert, "Spiritual Concepts Drawing a Different Breed." *The New York Times*, September 29, 1986, pp. 1, 29.

————, "Spiritual Go-betweens: A Growing Fad." *The New York Times*, May 9, 1987, p. 10.

———, "Teachings of 'Ramtha' Pull Hundreds West." *The New York Times*, November 16, 1986, pp. 1, 10.

McQuay, David, "Trance Channeling, A Hotline to Universal Truth?" *The Sunday Denver Post Magazine*, June 23, 1985, p. 1.

Montgomery, Ruth, and Joanne Garland, *Herald of the New Age.* New York: Fawcett Crest, 1986.

Ostrander, Sheila, and Lynn Schroeder, *Handbook of PSI Discoveries.* New York: Berkley Books, 1974.

———"She's Having the Time of Her Lives." *People Magazine*, January 26, 1987, pp. 29–35.

Publishers Weekly, Obituary, October 16, 1984, p. 29.

Ramtha, with Douglas J. Mahr, *Voyage to the New World.* New York: Fawcett Gold Medal, 1985.

Regush, Nicholas, and Jan Merta, *Exploring the Human Aura.* New Jersey: Prentice-Hall, 1975.

Reilly, Harold J., *The Edgar Cayce Handbook for Health.* New York: Macmillan, 1975.

Riva, Pam, "Trance Séances Given at United Nations HQ." *Psychic News*, December 17, 1983, pp. 1, 7.

Roberts, Jane, *Adventures in Consciousness.* New Jersey: Prentice-Hall, 1975.

———, *The God of Jane.* New Jersey: Prentice-Hall, 1981.

———, *Psychic Politics.* New Jersey: Prentice-Hall, 1976.

———, *A Seth Book: The "Unknown" Reality.* New Jersey: Prentice-Hall, 1986.

———, *Seth Speaks.* New York: Bantam Books, 1972.

Rodegast, Pat, and Judith Stanton, *Emmanuel's Book.* Weston, Connecticut: Friend's Press, 1985.

Roman, Sanaya, and Duane Packer, *Opening to Channel: How to Connect with Your Guide.* Oakland, California: LuminEssence Productions, 1987.

———, "Learn to Channel: A Spirit Guide." Tiburon, California: H. J. Kramer, 1987.

Sharma, Ishwar Chandra, *Cayce, Karma and Reincarnation.* Wheaton, Illinois: Quest, 1975.

Silverstein, Bonnie, "Cézanne through a Psychic." *American Artist*, April 1983, pp. 79–81.

Stevens, Jay, "When the Spirit World Touched Chittenden." *Yankee Magazine*, January 1987, pp. 78–83, 124.

Young, Stanley, "Body Doubles?" *Los Angeles Magazine*, December 1986, pp. 100–104.

———, "Same Channel Next Week." *Whole Earth Review*, Fall 1986, pp. 90–92.